100

From Rinks to Regiments

HOCKEY HALL-OF-FAMERS
AND THE GREAT WAR

Alan Livingstone MacLeod

HERITAGE

VICTORIA · VANCOUVER · CALGARY

Heritage House Publishing Company Ltd.
heritagehouse.ca

Cataloguing information available from Library and Archives Canada

978-1-77203-268-0 (pbk)
978-1-77203-269-7 (epub)

Edited by Lesley Cameron
Proofread by Stephen Harries
Cover and interior design by Jacqui Thomas
Front cover and title page image: 228th Battalion Hockey Juniors
Back cover images (top to bottom): Percy LeSueur (1911–12 C55 series), Moose Goheen (1960–61 Topps All-Time Greats), Harry "Punch" Broadbent (1912–13 C57 series), Alex Connell (1933–34 V252 Canadian Gum series)

Unless otherwise indicated, images displayed in this book are the author's own, or else are of hockey memorabilia or archival items in his personal collections or are photographs in the public domain.

The interior of this book was produced on 100% post-consumer recycled paper, processed chlorine free, and printed with vegetable-based inks.

We acknowledge the financial support of the Government of Canada through the Canada Book Fund (CBF) and the Canada Council for the Arts, and the Province of British Columbia through the British Columbia Arts Council and the Book Publishing Tax Credit.

22 21 20 19 18 1 2 3 4 5

Printed in Canada

In memory of John "Junior" Hanna,
New York Rangers (1958–61),
Montreal Canadiens (1963–64),
Philadelphia Flyers (1967–68).
Not a Hall-of-Famer, but an enduring hockey
hero to a long-ago Cape Breton boy.

CONTENTS

Preface

On October 7, 1959—opening day of the 1959–60 National Hockey League (NHL) season—a twelve-year-old boy penned a letter to Clarence Campbell, president of the NHL. He politely asked Mr. Campbell for a list of the rosters of the six NHL teams, the names and uniform numbers of every player. Within a few days, an envelope bearing the NHL logo arrived in the kid's mailbox. Mr. Campbell had complied with the boy's request. The kid would repeat his request on the following year's opening day and again on the one after that.

From the vantage point of the adult the boy would eventually become, the kid looks like someone who must surely have been one of the most devoted hockey fans of his time. He knew by heart the names and uniform numbers of every NHL player—all those who skated for his beloved Montreal Canadiens, every one of the despised Toronto Maple Leafs. He knew them all.

He was a newspaper delivery boy and used the proceeds of his labours to buy a subscription to *The Hockey News*, the hockey bible. The *News* was printed on newsprint in tabloid format and generally arrived by mail on the same day every week during the winter. The boy keenly anticipated the mailman's arrival.

It wasn't just Clarence Campbell who received the kid's letters. He wrote to le Club de hockey Canadien and asked for signed photographs of all the players—the magnificent Beliveau and all the others. It would never happen today, but the boy got what he asked for. A package arrived by return mail containing black-and-white photographs of all Les Habs—Beliveau, Rocket Richard, Dickie Moore, all of them.

The boy spent the summers of 1958 and '59 with his grandmother on the outskirts of Saint-Lambert on the opposite side of the St. Lawrence River from Montreal. One day during his 1959 stay, he learned that a group of Canadiens were to play a charity softball game against a local team. He figured out which bus would get him to the scene of this wondrous event. He took his autograph book. Several of the Canadiens signed it—including future Hall-of-Famers Doug Harvey and Dickie Moore.

In 1960, a bright light among the Shirriff dessert people came up with an ingenious plan for gaining an edge over their competitors at Jell-O. They decided to launch a promotion aimed at inducing hockey-loving boys to switch their dessert allegiance from Jell-O to Shirriff. In time for the 1960–61 season, the company included plastic discs featuring the images of NHL hockey players in the packaging of their jelly desserts—120 "hockey coins" in all, twenty for each of the six teams of the NHL at that time.

The kid asked the nice ladies along his paper route if they might be persuaded to buy Shirriff desserts for their families and save the hockey coins for him. The ladies agreed. In short order he had all 120 hockey

Jean Beliveau/1960–61.
Shirriff Dessert Hockey Coins

ALL-TIME GREATS

LESTER PATRICK

Lester Patrick/1960–61.
Topps All-Time Greats series

coins. He didn't realize it at the time, but his powers of persuasion were as great as they would ever be.

In the autumn of 1960, the folks at the Topps bubble gum company produced a hockey card set featuring something entirely unique. Twenty-seven of the cards in the set featured all-time greats of the game, men whose playing days had occurred decades earlier, some before the turn of the century. Few of the players were familiar to the boy, but their names were evocative—Paddy Moran, Dickie Boone, Dit Clapper, Cyclone Taylor. The first card in the series was assigned to a man whose name arises many times in this book—Lester Patrick. Eventually, every one of those twenty-seven players would be inducted in the Hockey Hall of Fame.

When he saw this series of hockey cards, the boy realized the game had a *history*. And judging by the names of the all-time greats, the uniforms they wore, and the brief biographical notes on the back of the cards, the history was likely to be intriguing.

A few years later he spotted an ad in *The Hockey News* for a book called *Official N.H.L. Record Book 1917–64*. It was sold for a measly buck twenty-five. He sent away for it, and when it arrived, he pored over it, learning more about the all-time greats.

The kid is now grown tall, but he still consults the old record book. He still owns the 1960–61 All-Time Greats cards, the signed Montreal Canadiens images, the Shirriff hockey coins.

Many worthy mothers got rid of their boys' hockey cards when the lads grew up and seemed no longer interested in the items that were once so precious, but the paperboy's mum was special: she kept the whole lot. A time came when her son wanted to see them again. The boyhood relics, every one of them, were waiting for him.

Doubtless there were many other kids across the country who learned from the 1960 All-Time Greats cards that their favourite game had a history. Perhaps they learned that for several of the greats born in the 1890s, their history as players would intersect with history of a very different sort: the cataclysm of the Great War.

Leafing through the All-Time Greats, kids in Winnipeg might have discovered they shared a birthplace with Frank Fredrickson, a war-time flier who subsequently led Canada to its first Olympic hockey gold medal. Kids in Brantford, Ontario, might have been introduced to Bill Cook, who won a medal for gallantry in the war and went on to a storied career with the New York Rangers. Kids living in Russell, Manitoba, perhaps encountered Mervyn Dutton, a man from their home town who, despite nearly losing a leg at Vimy Ridge, went on to become a Hockey Hall-of-Famer and NHL president.

This is a book for all the hockey-loving kids of 1960 and everyone else curious about a group of young men, now largely forgotten, and the fascinating stories about their careers as elite hockey players and soldiers of the Great War.

—1—

The present year, 2018, marks the centenary of two events of significance to many Canadians, one of them weighty, the other an enduring source of delight for much of the country. The catastrophe that was the Great War came to its end a century ago in November 1918. That same year, the first season of the National Hockey League concluded with Reg Noble leading the Toronto Arenas to the NHL championship over Joe Malone and the Montreal Canadiens.

T his is a book treating the nexus—*collision* might be a better term—between hockey and war.

Thirty players enshrined in the Hockey Hall of Fame—all of them elite players of their time—also served as soldiers in the Great War, most of them in the Canadian Expeditionary Force—the Canada Corps that distinguished itself in now-mythic Belgian and French battlefields, Ypres, the Somme, Vimy, Passchendaele. In addition to those thirty players, another two luminaries—one referee, one builder—served as soldiers and are featured in this book.

Even people who care little about hockey recognize the names Gordie Howe, Bobby Orr, and Wayne Gretzky—each of them an exalted member of the Hockey Hall of Fame. But there are other Hall-of-Famers—men just as celebrated in their time as Sidney Crosby and Connor McDavid are today—who have been largely or entirely forgotten even by keen hockey fans. How many hockey enthusiasts could tell an inquirer a single thing about Harry Trihey, Jack Ruttan, or Moose Goheen? Phat Wilson, Harry Watson, or Frank Rankin? Each of these six is an honoured Hall-of-Famer, admired in his day as an elite hockey performer.

Given that this is a book about hockey, it is serendipitous that the men featured in these pages can be placed in three convenient periods: those born between 1877 and 1891, those born between 1892 and 1895, and those born after 1895. The first group principally comprises men who played most or all of their hockey as amateurs before the war years. Most of the players in the second group had careers that straddled the war—those men played hockey before 1915 then returned to hockey afterward, many of them turning professional. For the majority of men in the third group, their playing performance peaked in the postwar years, when most—but not all—of them were paid to play.

The first group played in an era very different from the one that followed the establishment of the NHL in 1917. In 1893, when Lord Stanley, Canada's sixth Governor-General, provided an impressive piece of silverware to reward the best hockey team in all the land, hockey was an entirely amateur affair. There was no such thing as a pro hockey player, no one who turned a preferred pastime into a livelihood. During the 1890s and in the first decade of the twentieth century, those playing the game did so for fun.

Hockey seasons of 110, 120 years ago were nothing like the eight- or nine-month marathons typical of the modern NHL. Teams might play as few as ten games in a scheduled season, perhaps even fewer. Gordie Howe played

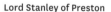

Lord Stanley of Preston

2,421 games in thirty-two major league seasons. There are players from hockey's early era who earned a place in the Hall of Fame having played a mere 175 games —or 55, or 38, or 32.

There was, of course, no television in hockey's early days. No Internet. Not even radio. But elite players were every bit as famous and ballyhooed in their time as the best of today's hockey heroes. They were celebrated in newspapers, by fans who attended their games, and by word of mouth.

Some of the feats of the greatest names in hockey of that time were truly prodigious. In 1976, Darryl Sittler of the Toronto Maple Leafs scored six goals in a single NHL game, one short of the league record seven achieved fifty-six years earlier by Joe Malone of the Quebec Bulldogs. In January 1905—twelve years before there was an NHL— the great Frank McGee scored fourteen goals in a single Stanley Cup game against the Dawson City Nuggets. *Fourteen*.

In 1924, Harry Watson led Canada to its second Olympic gold medal, scoring thirty-six goals in just five games. In three of those games the Canadian Olympians outscored their European opponents by an aggregate 85–0.

In 1928, goaltender Alex Connell shut out his NHL opposition in six straight games. Twice in his career, at a time when the regular schedule ran to only forty-four games, he recorded fifteen shutouts in a single season. His career goals-against average was 1.91—fewer than two goals a game. All three achievements are still NHL records nine decades later.

The Stanley Cup eventually became the Holy Grail of professional hockey, but in the beginning—and for close to two decades—Lord Stanley's silver bowl was the ultimate reward for men who played as amateurs.

The early game was very different from the one that evolved into what we see in NHL arenas today. In its initial years, hockey was a seven-man game, the *rover* being neither a forward nor a defenceman but someone who roamed the entire ice surface looking for opportunities to advantage his team. There was no such thing at that time as the forward pass—that was illegal—or a twenty-man roster divided into three or more shifts sharing the workload throughout a sixty-minute game. The early seven-man game typically featured just that—seven men who played the entire game without relief.

Hockey leagues—both amateur and professional—proliferated in the first decade and a half of the twentieth century. After 1910, many of them were professional: league operators and team owners *paid* for the services of the best players and competed vigorously to attract the ones considered the best of all.

In 1910, the National Hockey Association (NHA) established itself as the elite league in eastern Canada. A year later, brothers Lester and Frank Patrick established a rival top-tier pro league in the west: the Pacific Coast Hockey Association (PCHA).

1910 Renfrew Creamery Kings,
brothers **Lester** and **Frank Patrick**, centre

Long before players effectively became indentured to a single team, the NHA and PCHA engaged in bidding wars to lure the star players. A few years after the PCHA was founded, a second western circuit, the Western Canada Hockey League (WCHL), was established, and the marketplace for players' services tilted still further in the players' favour. Players enjoyed an ability to play for whomever they wanted at whatever price they could command. Players would never enjoy such freedom or control again.

When the Patrick brothers created the PCHA in 1911, they did so in a spirit of innovation and enterprise. The brothers built artificial-ice arenas in Victoria and Vancouver, the first of their kind in Canada, and the blue line, forward pass, penalty shot, and changing-on-the-fly were all introduced by them.

In 1917, the NHL launched itself from a different sort of platform. It was devised by owners of the NHA as a scheme to do an end-run around one of their fellow owners, Toronto's vexatious Eddie Livingstone. More than anything else, the NHL was founded as a device to get Eddie Livingstone out of their hair.

But despite its somewhat inglorious birth, the NHL grew into the most popular and powerful professional hockey league in the world.

From 1927 onwards, the Stanley Cup effectively became something never intended by Lord Stanley: the private property of the National Hockey League. Before that, for a period of twelve seasons from 1914 to 1926, it was up for grabs by the team prevailing in an annual showdown between the best team from the NHA (or NHL after 1917) in the east and the best in the west. There was no Stanley Cup confrontation in 1919 because of the Spanish influenza pandemic; in nine of twelve seasons it was the eastern team that prevailed, which resulted in the NHA/NHL's claiming its brand was superior. But many of the players who appear in the Second and Third Periods of this book played on both sides of the east-west divide.

All of the men in this book were inducted in the Hockey Hall of Fame between 1945 and 1970. The selection process for determining who is admitted to the Hockey Hall of Fame is very different from its counterpart in baseball. In baseball, every player who plays in the major leagues for ten years is automatically included in the annual Hall of Fame ballot five years after retirement.

The baseball voters—mostly writers in the major league cities—vote for those they consider worthy of inclusion in the Hall. The voting numbers are not secret: they are announced for all the world to see. Players blessed by 75 percent of the voters are admitted to the Hall of Fame. Those approved by at least 5 percent of the voters get another chance the following year. Those attracting votes from fewer than 5 percent of the voters are struck from the ballot.

In hockey, a selection committee is appointed to decide who gets into the Hall of Fame. The committee meets behind closed doors, and its deliberations are secret, as a matter of explicit policy. Players approved for induction are named and admitted to the Hall. Nothing is disclosed about the process of selection or rejection.

The current selection committee is a group of eighteen former players and team and NHL officials. One might wonder how much these arbiters of future Hall of Fame admissions could tell you about Harry Trihey or Frank Rankin, or how many would vote in favour of preserving Jack Ruttan's place in the Hall of Fame if they had the mandate to decide otherwise.

It seems highly likely that many of the old-time players wouldn't stand a chance of being voted into the Hall by the present Hockey Hall of Fame selection committee. The forgotten old guys didn't play enough games or score enough goals or win enough Stanley Cups to meet today's standards.

But seventy-three years ago, as the Second World War was concluding in 1945—just twenty-seven years after the Great War had ended—the Hockey Hall of Fame selection committee of its day had no hesitation in deciding that Frank McGee and Hobey Baker belonged in both its pantheon and its first draft.

Not every man in the Hockey Hall of Fame who was born in that era became a soldier. And given what was eventually known about the horrific conditions in which soldiers fought and died, it is easy to understand why a young man would prefer to play hockey on his home turf than fight in the mud and mire of Flanders. Canada was not under attack. Why should a young fellow join a European war that had nothing to do with him?

But there was enormous societal pressure on men to do their "duty" for King and Country. Those who declined to enlist—who chose to let others do the fighting—were reviled. As the war raged in Europe, young men still in Canada were accosted by women on city streets and given white feathers, marking them as shirkers and cowards. Among the Hockey Hall of Fame players born between 1885 and 1898, twenty-three did as Prime Minister Robert Borden wanted: they enlisted. An almost identical number—twenty-four—did not. They never served, either as volunteers or as conscripts.

This reflected what was happening in the country as a whole. While hundreds of thousands enlisted, just as many did not. In 1917, Borden and his Cabinet colleagues enacted conscription—and nearly tore the country apart as a consequence.

From a population of about eight million, more than 600,000 Canadians served in the Great War. About a tenth of them—more than sixty thousand—died. A cosmos of grief engulfed the mothers and fathers who lost a son, or two, or three. The parents of Frank McGee suffered the loss of two sons. Neither has a known grave. Frank and Charles are remembered on the same panel of the Vimy monument.

Four Hall-of-Famers—three Canadians, one American—paid the ultimate price for doing their duty. Others survived the war but were nonetheless its casualties: one nearly lost a leg at Vimy Ridge, another was seriously wounded by poison gas at Passchendaele.

Apart from their status as elite hockey players, the men of the Hockey Hall of Fame who served in the war are a microcosm: a cross-section of the entire body of men—both ordinary and remarkable—who fought for Canada between 1914 and 1918.

Five of the early Hall-of-Famers were legitimate war heroes, decorated for bravery in the field. But by no means were they *all* war heroes. Twenty-eight of the thirty-two men featured in these pages volunteered as soldiers, while four were conscripted into the Canada Corps under the provisions of the 1917 *Military Service Act*.

They were not all model citizens either. They didn't always conform to the moral standards their mothers had urged upon them. During the war, one in every nine Canadian soldiers was hospitalized for sexually transmitted infections, or venereal disease (VD), as it was known at the time, an infection rate said to be even worse than that of the Australians and far greater than the number hospitalized for treatment of influenza during the same period. That ratio is almost exactly reflected among the group of thirty players in this book: Three of the thirty were for a time taken out of action to be treated for VD.

The allure of the Hockey Hall-of-Famers who were also soldiers in the war is not that they were all heroes and model citizens—whether in life or in good fiction, perfectly virtuous characters are never as compelling as those afflicted with fascinating flaws. It is the *stories* that are uncovered by delving into their war service records and their playing careers that are compelling—stories such as those of the player who survived the torpedoing of his ship, led Canada to its first hockey gold medal at Antwerp in 1920, and became Albert Einstein's friend.

Or the player whose over-the-top Chicago fans included the gangster Al Capone. Or the man decorated for gallantry in the war who was as fearless a referee as he was a soldier. Or the player beloved in New York as Ivan the Terrible, who surpassed even Gordie Howe's achievements by playing his last hockey season at age fifty-six.

My aim in this book is to bring to light the extraordinary stories of men who were not only remarkable hockey players but also soldiers of the Great War. By any measure of character and colour, these largely forgotten men are as worthy of their place in the Hall of Fame as the celebrated hockey heroes of modern times.

— 2 —

FIRST PERIOD

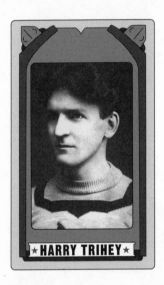

★ HARRY TRIHEY ★

The Irish in
Harry Trihey

Montreal Shamrocks (1896–1901)

199th Battalion Duchess of Connaught's Own Irish Rangers (1916–17)

Hockey Hall of Fame (1950)

★ ★ ★

The Stanley Cup, now the exclusive chattel of the National Hockey League (NHL), was a gift from Canada's sixth Governor-General, Lord Preston of Stanley, the Queen's representative in Ottawa from 1886 to 1893. While ensconced in Ottawa with their regal dad, Lord Stanley's sons, Arthur and Edward, enthusiastically embraced Canadian ways and in a short while became hockey players of some distinction. This serendipity resulted in Lord Stanley and his wife becoming keen hockey fans. Doubtless without any premonition of the significance it would come to have in the fullness of time, Lord Stanley thought it might be a nice idea to establish a trophy for the country's best amateur hockey clubs. Thus was born the Stanley Cup, first awarded in 1893 to the Montreal Hockey Club.

1889 Ottawa Rideau Rebels, **Arthur Stanley**, second left, standing; **Edward Stanley**, seated, front left

Harry Trihey is a member of the Hockey Hall of Fame principally on the strength of two dominant seasons as on-ice leader of the Montreal Shamrocks of the Canadian Amateur Hockey League (CAHL). Harry—named Henry Judah by his parents—was a real, live Christmas gift. Born December 25, 1877, by the age of seventeen he was already a player of some renown in Quebec amateur hockey circles. By 1898, he was the star of the Montreal Shamrocks, the pride and joy of Montreal's hockey-loving Irish community.

Hockey was a very different game in Lord Stanley's day from the game Canadians have come to obsess about in modern times. There were no professionals back then: players skated, shot, and scored for the pure joy of it. Teams iced seven skaters, including the rover, although he would fall by the wayside in just a few years. The men on each side would typically play *the entire game* with no substitutions. It is just as well,

1889 Montreal Shamrocks, **Hary Trihey**, centre, seated

perhaps, that the regular season was not the interminable eighty-two–game marathon it is today. In the 1898–99 season, the Shamrocks and their adversaries in the CAHL played only eight games apiece.

Five teams competed in the 1898–99 CAHL season—three were based in Montreal, one in Ottawa, one in Quebec City. Harry Trihey's Shamrocks led the way, winning seven of their eight games. The Quebec team had a perfect record—*losing* all eight of theirs. The Shamrocks' star during the regular season was Harry Trihey. He scored nineteen goals in the seven games he played, a rate of more than 2.5 per game. In one remarkable game against the hapless Quebec club, on February 4, 1899, Trihey scored *ten* goals. The Shamrocks were awarded the

Stanley Cup for their achievement. Just ten days later, they faced their first challenge for the Stanley Cup, from the Queen's University team. It was a challenge the Shamrocks easily met: they dismissed the Queen's skaters 6–2, with Trihey scoring three of the Montrealers' goals.

In 1899–1900, Harry Trihey outdid himself. The Shamrocks again dominated the regular season, once more winning seven of their eight scheduled games, with Trihey leading the way with seventeen goals in his seven starts. But it was in the ensuing Stanley Cup playoffs that Trihey cinched his future place in the Hockey Hall of Fame. In just five games, first three against the Winnipeg Victorias and then two against the Halifax Crescents, he scored twelve goals, leading the Shamrocks to dominant victories. He would play another effective season with the Shamrocks, but neither he nor the team would shine quite as brightly again.

Trihey stayed in the game as a referee, club executive, and advisor, but it was in other fields that he made his later mark. He became a successful lawyer in Montreal, and then, in 1914, the war broke out.

Trihey was a key player in the mobilization of an infantry battalion—an Irish-themed one, of course—named the 199th Battalion Duchess of Connaught's Own Irish Rangers, and its first commanding officer. The all-Irish battalion was assured that it would be held intact, kept together for action at the Western Front of Flanders and France. It was the sort of promise made to many infantry battalions; the 199th was neither the first nor the last to see

Lieutenant-Colonel Harry Trihey

such a promise broken. The 199th was absorbed into a reserve battalion with the intention that its men would be used to reinforce front-line units decimated by what was frequently termed "the wastage of war."

Lieutenant-Colonel Harry Trihey hit the roof. He resigned his commission. The *New York Post* published a blistering letter he wrote savaging both the British and the Canadian military authorities for the broken promise. The letter was then published in the Montreal newspapers. The military brass was so unimpressed they considered bringing sedition charges against Trihey. However, perhaps because of the reputation he had established as a hockey star in Montreal—but more likely thanks to the friends he had made as an officer of the Quebec court— Trihey dodged a bullet. There was no court-martial, no sedition trial.

Harry Trihey was inducted in the Hockey Hall of Fame in 1950, a little too late for him to get any satisfaction from the honour. He had died in Montreal eight years before, in 1942, sixteen days short of his sixty-fifth birthday.

McGee, Gilmour,
and the Sublime Silver Seven

★ FRANK McGEE ★

FRANK McGEE

Ottawa Silver Seven (1902–06)

21st (Eastern Ontario) Battalion (1915–16)

Hockey Hall of Fame (1945)

★ ★ ★

★ BILLY GILMOUR ★

BILLY GILMOUR

Ottawa Silver Seven/
McGill Redmen/Montreal Victorias/
Ottawa Senators (1902–16)

1st Construction Battalion (1916–18)

Hockey Hall of Fame (1962)

★ ★ ★

1905 Ottawa Silver Seven, **Billy Gilmour**, second right, standing; **Frank McGee**, far right

W hen Harry Trihey scored an astonishing ten goals in a single game in February 1899, knowledgeable observers might have concluded that no hockey player would ever match his achievement. It took fewer than five years for such a prediction to be undone. On January 16, 1905, Frank McGee matched Trihey's ten goals—then scored four more for the Ottawa Silver Seven in a Stanley Cup playoff game against the Dawson City Nuggets. The Nuggets may have been the pride of their storied Klondike city, but thanks to McGee's fourteen goals, the Shamrocks outclassed them 23–2 on this humiliating day.

The Silver Seven club was an early hockey dynasty, winners of the Stanley Cup in four consecutive seasons from 1902–03 to '05–06.

Frank McGee was the shining star of this elite team that would eventually have six of its players inducted in the Hockey Hall of Fame, three of whom would step forward to do their duty for King and Country in the Great War.

Francis (Frank) Clarence McGee was the scion of a prominent Ottawa family. His uncle, Thomas D'Arcy McGee, was a Canadian Father of Confederation and a Cabinet minister in John A. Macdonald's government. D'Arcy McGee was killed by an assassin's bullet in 1868; a government building in the nation's capital is named in his honour.

McGee was twenty-two when he first won the Stanley Cup. His apparent on-ice perfection gave no hint that he played with a significant disability: he accomplished all his prodigious goal-scoring despite having only one functioning eye. While still a teenager, he had lost the sight in his left eye as a result of an injury sustained while playing hockey. It did not stop him. With the use of just one eye, McGee outshone virtually every other player with two: in just six regular-season games with the 1902–03 Ottawa club, McGee led the team in scoring with fourteen goals. He did the same in subsequent seasons: over a four-year span, McGee scored seventy-one goals in just twenty-three games. He was just as effective in Stanley Cup playoffs during the same time frame, with sixty-four goals in twenty-two games.

The Silver Seven juggernaut was very much a family affair. Frank McGee's older brother, Jim, was his teammate on the 1903–04 club and might well have shared in additional Stanley Cup glory had he not been killed in a riding accident in May 1904, just two days short of his twenty-fifth birthday.

Billy Gilmour was Frank McGee's teammate for the first three of McGee's Stanley Cup runs. Two other Gilmour brothers, Suddy and Dave, were also Ottawa stars. In the 1903–04 season, the three Gilmours trailed only McGee among the leading Silver Seven scorers.

Billy Gilmour, four years younger than his teammate, was only eighteen when he began his hockey collaboration with McGee. During his time playing with the Silver Seven and his McGill College team,

Lieutenant Frank McGee

Gilmour also completed a degree in engineering. While worthy enough to earn him an eventual place in the Hockey Hall of Fame, his numbers were not quite as impressive as McGee's: forty-two goals in forty-seven regular-season games, and another seven in his nine Stanley Cup playoff games.

When the Great War broke out in 1914, and with their glory days as hockey stars behind them, Frank McGee and Billy Gilmour did as thousands of other men and boys were doing: they enlisted in the Canadian Expeditionary Force (CEF). McGee was the first to join, enlisting in the 21st Infantry Battalion in November 1914. By this time he was a thirty-four-year-old Ottawa civil servant. As with hockey, the war was also a family affair for the McGees. Frank's older brother, Charles Edward, had enlisted in September 1914; he was killed in action at Festubert the following May. Another brother, Walter Robert, also went off to war—and lived to tell the tale.

Concerned that his left-eye blindness might disqualify him for service in the CEF, Frank pulled a fast one—or *thought* he did. During the eyesight portion of his medical examination, he covered his bad eye and then used his opposite hand to cover the same eye when instructed to switch sides by the examining doctor. McGee's war service record seems to make it clear that the doctor wasn't duped: he recorded McGee as having good vision in the right eye and left the rest of the eyesight section in his report form blank. Despite his bad eye, the old hockey hero was welcomed in the CEF with the rank of lieutenant.

Meanwhile, given his standing as a professional engineer, Gilmour received a lieutenant's commission in the 1st Construction Battalion. Men serving in a construction battalion faced considerably less danger than those who did their duty as infantrymen. Gilmour went through the war without serious incident and returned home, whole and unbroken, in 1919.

McGee had a different experience. In late 1915, he was seriously wounded when the armoured car he was handling was blown into a ditch by a high explosive shell. His right knee was damaged, and the wound and related complications took him out of action for months. Once he had healed, McGee was given the opportunity to take on a headquarters role and stay out of harm's way. Instead, he chose to return to his battalion on the front lines—just in time to join the Canadian fight for the village of Courcelette in the bloody Battle of the Somme.

September 16, 1916—just twelve days after McGee had rejoined his battalion—was a lethal day in the Canada Corps. Some 453 Canadian soldiers perished on that single day, including ten men from the 21st Battalion. Frank McGee's body was one of 298 from that day that was never recovered and identified; his name is one of more than eleven

Vimy Monument

thousand inscribed on Canada's Great War memorial at Vimy Ridge, a tribute to Canadians who died fighting in France and have no known grave. He is not the only family member remembered here—he is commemorated on the same Vimy panel as his brother Charles.

Though Frank McGee is no longer as famed as he was in the early 1900s, the proof that he is among the all-time greats of the game is reflected in this: he is one of the inaugural group of players inducted in the Hall of Fame, one of the first eleven enshrined in 1945.

As for Billy Gilmour, he returned to Montreal after the war and continued his career as a professional engineer. He died in 1959, a few days before his seventy-fourth birthday. Like Harry Trihey, he would never know about the honour bestowed upon him. His induction in the Hall of Fame came about in 1962, three years after his death.

Peerless Percy LeSueur
Maestro in Hockey and Bayonet Fighting

1911–12 C55 series

**Smiths Falls Seniors/
Ottawa Senators/
Toronto Shamrocks/
Toronto Blueshirts** (1903–16)

134th Battalion/228th Battalion (1916–18)

Hockey Hall of Fame (1961)

★ ★ ★

In March 1906, twenty-four-year-old Percy LeSueur experienced a good news– bad news sort of season tending goal for the Smiths Falls Seniors of the Federal Amateur Hockey League. The Smiths Falls lads had enjoyed an unblemished record during the FAHL regular season, winning all seven of their scheduled games against opponents from Ottawa, Cornwall, Brockville, and Montreal. Percy's teammates scored thirty-five goals against their foes, while Percy allowed only thirteen to get past him—an average of barely two a game.

On the strength of their FAHL supremacy, the Smiths Falls boys qualified to challenge the defending Stanley Cup champions, the

Ottawa Senators—the mighty Silver Seven. That is when the bad news arose. Led by their luminous star, Frank McGee, the Ottawa side dominated Smiths Falls. Even with Percy LeSueur in goal, Smiths Falls lost to the Silver Seven at Ottawa's Dey's Arena. In the first game of a best-of-three series, Smiths Falls lost narrowly, 6–5. In the second game, Ottawa had a field day, humbling their opponents 8–2.

Strangely enough, the Ottawa players were impressed with the young netminder who had failed to stop eight of their shots. Under the Stanley Cup rules prevailing at the time, it was only a matter of days before the Ottawa team faced *another* challenge, this time from the Montreal Wanderers. The Montrealers had finished the Eastern Canada Amateur Hockey Association regular season with a record identical to Ottawa's—nine wins against a single loss. A two-game, total-point series would determine the ECAHA championship—and the next holder of the Stanley Cup.

1911 Ottawa Senators, **Percy LeSueur**, centre

Just six days after dispatching Smiths Falls, the Silver Seven faced off against the Wanderers and got a taste of their own medicine—they lost ignominiously in the first game, 9–1. Ottawa decided it required a change in personnel and called upon none other than Percy LeSueur to take over in goal. LeSueur agreed, and there ensued perhaps the greatest comeback in Stanley Cup history.

Game 2—March 17, 1906—was one for the ages. LeSueur surrendered an early goal, increasing the Ottawa deficit to ten. Then, led by McGee, the Silver Seven roared back, scoring ten straight goals to level the aggregate score at ten apiece. Sadly for Ottawa and LeSueur, there would be no Cinderella ending. Montreal's Lester Patrick scored two late goals, clinching the series for Montreal and ending Ottawa's four-year run as Stanley Cup kings.

That memorable game would be the only one in which McGee and LeSueur played as teammates. McGee would never play another game for Ottawa, and LeSueur was launched on a nine-year career as guardian of the Ottawa net. He soon acquired the moniker Peerless Percy and led Ottawa to victories in three Stanley Cup challenges between 1909 and 1911. LeSueur had redeemed himself. After being humbled in the Smiths Falls goal, he was now a star.

LeSueur was good at what he did—and he was good-looking too. The goaltender would find his allure exploited for commercial purposes. In the 1950s, a clever marketer discovered that combining bubble gum with bits of cardboard featuring the image of a hockey player was a sure-fire way to separate boys from their dimes and quarters. But four decades earlier, the same tactic had been used for the purpose of selling cigarettes and tobacco. Handsome Percy LeSueur's face appeared in at least three series of tobacco cards in the second decade of the 1900s.

By the time his run with the Ottawa club had run its course, LeSueur was thirty-two. He would have two more productive years as a hockey professional, with Toronto teams in the National Hockey Association (NHA), from 1914 to 1916. At that point, Canadian hockey enthusiasts were distracted by a major world event. War had broken out in Europe in 1914, and young men and boys had enlisted in their multitudes in the Canadian Expeditionary Force (CEF) and gone off to war for King and Country. In the early stages of the war, tens of thousands flocked to recruiting centres, keen not to miss their chance at a glorious role in the adventure many worried might be over by Christmas 1914. Two years of hellish warfare and appalling casualties changed all that, and by late 1916 the flow of new recruits was no longer keeping pace with the losses generated by the wastage of war.

In the quest to address its recruitment problems, the Canadian government considered various measures, both great and small. One of the great measures—one that very nearly tore the country apart in 1917—was conscription: compelling young men to go to war whether they wanted to or not.

Some bright light in the military establishment considered an alluring and far less draconian solution: Why not mobilize a group of talented hockey players to compete in the principal hockey league of the day, have them represent a battalion of the CEF, put them in a manly khaki-coloured uniform, have them succeed gloriously, and so induce young men to flock to the recruiting stations? Thus was born the 228th Battalion Northern Fusiliers, perhaps the most unusual major league hockey team there ever was.

The Fusiliers took to the ice in late December 1916, defeating the Ottawa Senators 10–7 in their first game. They followed that up with a 10–4 shellacking of the Montreal Wanderers and then beat Toronto 4–0. A very good start. Playing out of Toronto's Mutual Street Arena, the Fusiliers were soon the toast of the town, one of the major fan attractions in the league. But after ten games, just a single victory in arrears of the league leaders, the military bosses decided they needed soldiers more than they needed hockey players. After a mere month and a half in the NHA, the team was disbanded and the battalion shipped off to France.

One of the star players recruited for the Northern Fusiliers was Peerless Percy LeSueur. He appears in a group portrait of 228th players, all wearing military uniforms, but he did not actually tend goal while wearing the 228th hockey jersey. The military had another role for LeSueur, now aged thirty-four. He had originally enlisted in an infantry battalion, the 134th Battalion (48th Highlanders), but was later redeployed as a Divisional Headquarters instructor in physical training and bayonet fighting.

Was it his curriculum vitae as a hockey warrior and his first-hand experience with hooking, slashing, and spearing that qualified him for his new role? Perhaps. Whatever the reason, LeSueur was fortunate: instead of being consigned to the meat grinder of the Western Front, he remained in Canada and did his bit for the war effort by instructing foot soldiers in the fine art of dispatching the enemy by effective use of the bayonet. Unlike his one-game teammate Frank McGee, LeSueur was kept out of the killing fields of Flanders and France—and so survived.

Though he never played another professional game after 1916, LeSueur remained in hockey—as a referee, advisor, coach, historian, commentator, and journalist—for a long time. By the time he left the game, he could look back on a career in hockey that spanned half a century.

Percy St. Helier LeSueur was inducted in the Hockey Hall of Fame in 1961. In contrast to Harry Trihey and Billy Gilmour, he lived long enough to savour the honour, though not by much: he died the year afterward in Hamilton, Ontario, at age eighty.

George McNamara

and His Band of Brothers

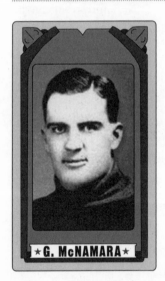

★ G. McNAMARA ★

**Canadian Soo/Montreal Shamrocks/
Waterloo Colts/Halifax Crescents/
Toronto Tecumsehs/Toronto HC/Toronto
Blueshirts/Toronto Shamrocks/228th Battalion**
(1906–17)

228th Battalion/6th Canadian Railway Troops
(1916–19)

Hockey Hall of Fame (1958)

★ ★ ★

The pride of Penetanguishene, Ontario, George McNamara was, by the standards of the early 1900s, a giant of a man—he stood more than six feet tall and weighed 220 pounds. For much of his playing career he was paired behind the blue line with his brother Howard, who at 240 pounds was even bigger than his fearsome brother. Though George was older than Howard by a few years, the scary siblings were dubbed the Dynamite Twins: they thrived on intimidating their hockey adversaries.

In an era when hockey leagues were sprouting like mushrooms all over Canada and the northern United States, George made his professional hockey debut as a twenty-year-old with the Canadian Soo in the 1906–07 season of the International Professional Hockey League (IPHL) against several U.S. teams—Sault Ste. Marie, Calumet, and Houghton in Michigan, and Pittsburgh, Pennsylvania.

In the early 1900s, pro hockey players were not the indentured serfs they would become at a later time; they had much greater freedom to come and go as they pleased and to play for whomever they liked. After his short stay in Canada's Sault Ste. Marie, George took his act to Montreal, where he played two seasons in the Eastern Canada Hockey Association (ECHA) with the Montreal Shamrocks—Harry Trihey's old club. The Shamrocks won only half their games in the 1907–08 season and just two of twelve the following year. It was in that losing season of '08–09 that the McNamara brothers were first paired, but despite the presence of the Dynamite Twins in the lineup, the 2–10 Shamrocks didn't convince anyone to switch their allegiance from the mighty Ottawa Silver Seven.

In 1910, George and Howard McNamara departed for Ontario and a season with the Waterloo Colts of the Ontario Professional Hockey League (OPHL). At that point they were joined by a *third* brother, Harold, just as rough and tough as the other two.

It was in Waterloo in 1910–11 that George gathered his first big hoard of press clippings. One of his teammates was a young future Hall-of-Fame luminary, Joe Malone. Malone was a nineteen-year-old Waterloo rookie that season, still a few seasons away from his career pinnacle. Though McNamara was a defenceman, not a forward, he managed to score fifteen goals in sixteen games, bettering Malone's season total by five goals.

The McNamara brothers took to the road again. In 1911–12, they breathed salt Atlantic air in Halifax, playing with the Crescents of the Maritime Professional Hockey League (MPHL), a four-team agglomeration of one club in Moncton, one in New Glasgow, and two in Halifax. The Crescents tied for last place.

Like the boll weevil of folk song fame, the McNamara brothers clearly still hadn't found a home: they moved again, and this time it was for good. Gear bags in hand, they departed for Toronto, and it was there that George McNamara spent the rest of his professional hockey days.

In 1912–13, the McNamaras took their first turn in the NHA, precursor to the NHL and the premier professional league of the day. In '12–13, the NHA comprised six clubs—one each in both Quebec and Ottawa, and two each in both Montreal and Toronto. Joe Malone was now no longer playing in George's shadow: he led the Quebec Bulldogs to the NHA regular-season title, scoring forty-two goals in twenty games. George and Howard McNamara were paired on the blue line of the Toronto Tecumsehs. The Tecumsehs finished last.

Then, finally, in 1913–14, George had his turn in the Stanley Cup spotlight. Playing with several teammates who would one day join him in the Hockey Hall of Fame, including two—Allan Davidson and Frank Foyston—featured in this book, George McNamara enjoyed his first taste of hockey glory. His team, the Toronto Hockey Club of the NHA, finished tied for the best regular-season record and then beat the Montreal Canadiens in the post-season to earn the Stanley Cup, which by this time had evolved into the top prize of professional hockey.

228th Battalion Hockey Juniors, **George McNamara**, centre, standing

In the final years of his professional career, George McNamara skated for three different Toronto franchises: the Blueshirts, Shamrocks, and, in 1916–17, that most unusual of pro hockey clubs we have already encountered, the 228th Battalion Northern Fusiliers.

Brothers in hockey, George and Howard would be brothers in arms too. In 1916, first George and then Howard enlisted in the Canadian Expeditionary Force, each determined to do his bit for the Canadian war effort. Each joined the 228th Battalion and each was given an officer's commission. As noted elsewhere, talented hockey players were recruited to the 228th to play hockey and wear a sweater in CEF khaki green bearing the 228th emblem. The plan was that the team's success on the ice would induce young men to join the war effort.

George McNamara was a leading light in the organization of the 228th hockey effort, although both brothers played on the 228th NHA team. George also coached a team of 228th men who were young enough to play in the Ontario Hockey Association (OHA) junior division. In a team portrait of the 228th junior squad, George, in his CEF officer's uniform, stands taller than all the young fellows under his charge.

The 228th players didn't have long to enjoy their respite from the guns of the Western Front. In mid-February 1917, less than two months after its hockey launch, the 228th was pulled out of the NHA and shipped overseas to wield rifles rather than hockey sticks. The McNamara brothers went willingly.

Captain George McNamara

In his enlistment documents, George had listed his "trade or calling" not as *hockey player* but as *contractor*. Given that a good number of the battalion's men had experience in railway construction and operation, the 228th was re-designated as the Sixth Canadian Railway Troops, and it was in that capacity—railway construction and repair—that the McNamaras and the other men of the battalion served for the rest of the war. George did well in the Sixth Canadian Railway Troops—he was mentioned in Dispatches, was promoted to major, and survived the war unscathed. In March 1919, after two years in France, Major McNamara returned to Canada.

His playing days were over, but there was still a role in hockey for George McNamara. The Stanley Cup had by now been appropriated by hockey professionals, and in 1909, a new trophy, the Allan Cup, was established to fill the role originally intended for Lord Stanley's Cup—the award bestowed annually on the best amateur team in the land. In 1924, George McNamara, now thirty-eight years old, coached the Sault Ste. Marie Greyhounds to an Allan Cup victory.

Partners in hockey and war, George and Howard were partners in business too. After the war, they established the McNamara Construction Company and built it into a thriving concern.

Given all they had shared as brothers, it might have been serendipitous had George and Howard both been awarded a place in the Hockey Hall of Fame but it was not to be. Only George would be accorded that honour. He was inducted in 1958, one of fourteen in that Hockey Hall of Fame draft, including eleven players in this book.

Like several other of the soldier-players, George McNamara never knew about the honour bestowed upon him. He had died six years earlier at age sixty-six. Howard wouldn't know of it either. He had died in 1940 at age fifty, predeceased by Harold, who had died at age forty-eight in 1937, in Peru, a long, long way from the Waterloo arena where he had shone on the ice with his brothers in 1911.

The Character of
George Richardson

★ G. RICHARDSON ★

**Queen's University/Kingston 14th Regiment/
Kingston Frontenacs** (1902–12)

2nd Battalion (Eastern Ontario Regiment)
(1914–16)

Hockey Hall of Fame (1950)

★ ★ ★

More than two hundred players have been honoured by induction in the Hockey Hall of Fame. All of them are athletes who distinguished themselves through on-ice talent and productivity, many of them over a long period of time. Seventeen played at least fifteen hundred regular-season games, nineteen scored at least six hundred goals, and seventeen were goaltenders who shut out the opposition in sixty games or more.

In the early years of the twentieth century, hockey was nothing like the industry it is now. Players played short seasons, often for the pure joy of the game rather than for profit.

George Richardson was inducted in the Hockey Hall of Fame long ago, with career totals of 108 goals in just thirty-eight regular-season and playoff games. Scoring at a rate of close to three goals a game, there is no doubt that Richardson was a supremely talented hockey player, but sometimes factors beyond mere talent and productivity have led electors to honour a player with a place in the Hall. If there were a wing in the Hall of Fame dedicated to men of exceptional *character*, no one would have a higher place in its pantheon than Richardson.

The son of a prominent and well-heeled family in Kingston, Ontario, Richardson studied at Queen's University between 1903 and 1906. He was still sixteen when he began his first year at Queen's. In addition to flourishing as a scholar, he shone as a hockey player too. Over a three-year span with the varsity squad, Richardson scored twenty-three goals in just a dozen games. Twice during this span

1905–06 Queen's University Hockey Team, **George Richardson**, seated behind trophy

Queen's was Canadian university hockey champion. At age seventeen, in 1903, he led his Queen's mates to victories over two U.S. university hockey powerhouses—Princeton and Yale—to win the all-North America intercollegiate title.

One of the tributes paid to Richardson the hockey player was that he was that rarest of men—a true gentleman on the ice. Assessed only thirty-five penalty minutes in his whole career, he twice went through a campaign recording no penalty minutes at all. On one memorable occasion he was called out for an infraction he had not committed. Rather than confronting the referee, he went to the penalty box and served his time without complaint. The referee later admitted he had blown the call—and apologized.

After graduating from Queen's, Richardson joined his family's grain-exporting firm but continued to play hockey. Like many young men of the era, he was active in a volunteer Canadian Militia unit. He led a hockey team representing that unit—the Kingston 14th Regiment —to the OHA senior championship in 1908. After a couple of stints with the Kingston Frontenacs of the OHA, Richardson stepped back from his playing career at the age of just twenty-five, but he carried on in an executive capacity and in 1911 helped lead the Frontenacs juniors to an OHA title.

All of his playing success in hockey was as an amateur: he never played a single game for money as a hockey professional.

When the Great War broke out in 1914, the former Queen's star player was an early volunteer in the CEF. He was given a commission as a lieutenant in an infantry battalion, the 2nd Battalion (Eastern Ontario Regiment) and went off to war. By February 1915 he was in the trenches near Armentières in northern France.

One of the early blood baths the Canada Corps endured was in and around the Belgian village of St. Julien in the spring of 1915. In just eleven days between April 24 and May 4, more than eleven hundred Canadians died in the fighting for St. Julien. The 2nd Battalion was one of the Canadian units decimated in the battle. George Richardson, now a captain, was wounded at St. Julien, but he survived—the only officer in his company left standing.

The better part of a year passed with Richardson remaining above the soil of Flanders. Then, on the night of February 8–9, 1916, Richardson ran out of luck. Under cover of night, a party of 2nd Battalion men commanded by Richardson had crept out toward enemy lines to lay explosives to destroy the enemy's barbed-wire entanglements.

1910–11 Kingston Frontenacs, **George Richardson,** third left; **Allan Davidson,** second right, middle row

The weather changed, raising the possibility that the Canadians might be observed from the German trenches. Richardson went out to lead his men and their explosives back to the Canadian lines. The Allies' worst fears were realized, as the Canadians were spotted. In the ensuing machine gun bursts, three were killed. Both of Richardson's hips were shattered and he suffered an abdominal wound as well. Within four hours he was dead of his wounds at age twenty-nine.

Captain Richardson was buried in Bailleul Communal Cemetery Extension, a few miles west of Lille. His is one of 290 Canadian burials among the 4,500 graves there. Almost all of the Canadians buried there died of wounds received in battle.

George Richardson's death caused great grief among those who loved him back in Canada, grief that may have been matched or even exceeded among the men and officers of the 2nd Battalion. It was said that Richardson would never ask his men to take a risk he wasn't prepared to take himself. He was wealthy—and unstinting in his willingness to spend his own money to improve the comfort and wellness of the men under his command. He paid for warm boots, gas masks, cigarettes, and more for his men out of his own pocket.

As much as he had relished being part of a team of successful hockey players, Richardson assigned even greater significance to his role as a military officer. "No matter what the future may bring," he wrote to his brother on one occasion, "there will never be a position, I know, which in the way of interest and personal pleasure will compare with the task of commanding a company."

Captain George Richardson

A 1917 article in the *Toronto Star* cited what one of Richardson's fellow officers said of his lost colleague: "No officer was ever more beloved by his men, who were ready to follow him anywhere. On his grave they put a wreath inscribed 'To one who played the game.'" He was posthumously awarded France's Legion of Honour.

Richardson's influence outlived him. His will reflected not just his wealth but his consideration and generosity too. He left $20,000 to Queen's, $30,000—more than $700,000 in current dollars—to Kingston charities, and another $30,000 to a trust fund for the education and welfare of the wives and children of the 2nd Battalion men who had served under him.

George Richardson's name lives on in Kingston. His brother James, the chancellor of Queen's from 1929 to 1939, donated the necessary funds to build the George Taylor Richardson Memorial Stadium in 1921. The stadium was replaced by a new building fifty years later; it still bears George Richardson's name.

In 1950, thirty-four years after he was killed in action, George Richardson was inducted in the Hockey Hall of Fame. Joining him in the 1950 draft were Harry Trihey and another player treated in this book, Scotty Davidson.

Richardson's Hockey Hall of Fame tablet describes him as "One of the great players of hockey's early days."

A great player, yes, and an exemplary human being too.

Jack Ruttan

At the Heart of Winnipeg Hockey

★ JACK RUTTAN ★

**University of Manitoba/
Winnipeg Hockey Club/
Winnipeg Somme** (1908–18)

**10th Canadian Mounted Rifles/
1st Pioneer Battalion** (1916–19)

Hockey Hall of Fame (1962)

★ ★ ★

Almost equidistant between Halifax and Victoria, the city of Winnipeg can lay legitimate claim to being at the heart of Canada—geographically and otherwise. Winnipeg has the smallest metropolitan population among the thirty NHL cities—and only half that of the second-smallest metropolis, but the city's fans are among the most loyal and supportive in the league. The franchise is one of the minority of NHL teams that regularly sells out all the seats on offer and accommodates another three hundred or so fans willing to pay to watch their team from the standing-room section.

It has always been thus. Winnipeggers have been passionate hockey fans virtually from the game's beginning. And why not? Winnipeg has no shortage of ice in winter. It was a Montreal club that first hoisted the Stanley Cup in victory—only to be vanquished by a team from Winnipeg. Between 1896 and 1902, seven Winnipeg teams were victorious in Stanley Cup challenges.

Winnipeg has produced many memorable hockey players, but one of the city's standouts is John Douglas "Jack" Ruttan, member of two hockey halls of fame—the better-known one in Toronto and its less familiar Manitoba counterpart in Winnipeg.

Ruttan had three years of amateur hockey stardom behind him when he entered the University of Manitoba in 1908. Despite playing as a defenceman, from behind the blue line, he was an accomplished scorer: in his U of M rookie year he scored ten goals in just seven games. A native-born Winnipegger, he did all of his hockey playing in the city, remaining an amateur in every game he ever played.

The highlight of his playing career occurred in 1913 when his Winnipeg Hockey Club won the Allan Cup, emblematic of senior amateur hockey supremacy in all Canada. En route to the Allan Cup, the Winnipegs vanquished the Moose Jaw Moose in a two-game series by the aggregate score 16–3, followed by an 18–8 conquest of the Edmonton Eskimos in the Cup final.

But for one brief return to the ice, Jack Ruttan's playing days were over by the time he was twenty-three, in 1914. A key factor in the derailment of his hockey career was the outbreak of the Great War in 1914. Ruttan had studied engineering at the University of Manitoba, and by the spring of 1915 he was a qualified civil engineer. Like many other young men, he entered the Canadian Expeditionary Force with experience as a part-time soldier—three years in the 100th Winnipeg Grenadiers and two with the 34th Fort Garry Horse. In April 1915, he enlisted at Grenfell, Saskatchewan, in the 10th Canadian Mounted Rifles. He was commissioned as a lieutenant.

Between 1914 and 1918 there were many ways to become a casualty of war. More than sixty thousand soldiers died in the war, the majority of them men who were killed in action or who died of their wounds, but a considerable minority perished less dramatically, of disease. Although Jack Ruttan did not die, he was plagued by disease throughout the war. His war service record includes a litany of conditions that obstructed his ability to participate as well as he might have wished: pharyngitis, appendicitis, anemia, weight loss, and a string of other ailments, the most serious of which was a duodenal ulcer.

At least one of the doctors who attended Ruttan blamed the ulcer, anemia, and weight loss on the "stress of campaign." Ruttan had crossed the Atlantic and reached France, but with all his time in sick bay he saw little or no front-line service. By now a captain, Ruttan was judged unfit for active service: the doctors recommended that he be sent back to Canada for home service.

The impact of the war, manifest in so many other ways on the home front, was evident in hockey too. For the 1917–18 season, a "patriotic league," the Winnipeg Military Hockey League was established, the team names reflecting major Canadian battles of the war—Winnipeg Ypres, Winnipeg Somme, Winnipeg Vimy. The best of the WMHL squads— the Winnipeg Ypres—made it all the way to the Allan Cup final in 1918, losing narrowly to the Kitchener Greenshirts, 6–4 in a two-game series.

Back in Winnipeg and medically unfit for duty at the Western Front, Ruttan played a principal role in the organization and operation of the WMHL in that 1917–18 season. He had one more go as an on-ice player, skating for the Winnipeg Somme in a single game.

Ruttan bounced back from his wartime health afflictions and kept a hand in the game. He coached his alma mater's hockey team at the University of Manitoba in 1923–24 and was active for many years after the war as a hockey referee and coach.

He played only thirty-two games of elite amateur hockey in his playing career, but on the strength of a "long and illustrious career in hockey" he was inducted in the Hockey Hall of Fame in 1962. Ruttan lived long enough to appreciate the honour: he lived to be eighty-four years of age, eventually dying—in Winnipeg, of course—in 1973.

Cooper Smeaton

Fearless Referee, Stanley Cup Trustee

★ C. SMEATON ★

18th Canadian Siege Battery (1917–19)

NHL Referee (1919–46)
Stanley Cup Trustee (1946–78)

Hockey Hall of Fame (1961)

★ ★ ★

James Cooper Smeaton was born in July 1890 at Carleton Place, Ontario, a little west of Ottawa. He shared his birthplace with Roy Brown, the ace fighter pilot initially credited for downing Manfred von Richthofen—The Red Baron—in the skies over the Western Front in April 1918.

Smeaton was still a toddler when his parents moved the family to Westmount, in Greater Montreal. Growing up in Westmount, young Cooper excelled in three sports—baseball, football, and hockey.

In 1910, he packed his bags for New York City, a proficient enough player to earn a spot with the 1910–11 New York Wanderers of the American Amateur Hockey Association (AAHA).

After his New York hiatus he returned to Montreal and took up a position with Sun Life Insurance Company. In 1908, he had taken on a sideline hockey role—referee. The sideline now became the specialty: Smeaton put aside his hockey stick for good and took up a referee's whistle. In 1913, then twenty-three years old, Smeaton was hired as a referee by the NHA.

Smeaton's mettle was tested very early by an accomplished hockey intimidator: Newsy Lalonde of the Montreal Canadiens. In one early game, Lalonde, a star player of his time, got in the rookie referee's face over a call Lalonde didn't like. But in the ensuing confrontation it was not Smeaton who blinked. Making best use of the authority assigned to referees at the time, he fined the star player—and sent him to the penalty box to boot. Lalonde never crossed Smeaton again.

The hockey culture prevailing at the time of the Great War was one modern-day officials might not readily recognize. Ordinarily it is the role of modern referees and linesmen to intervene in the brawls that sometimes erupt between rival players. In 1917, in a game involving the 228th Battalion Northern Fusiliers, Smeaton found himself as one of the *principals* in a fistfight—against Howard McNamara. On another occasion, while attending to an official's normal duty— breaking up a fight between players—Smeaton's intervention cost him three broken ribs.

Smeaton's experience in hand-to-hand fighting perhaps served him well in the next chapter of his life. In late May 1917, he enlisted at Montreal in an artillery unit of the Canadian Expeditionary Force (CEF)—the 3rd Draft Heavy and Siege Artillery. He was no longer a youngster by that time but a married man of twenty-six employed as a clerk with Sun Life. In his attestation, he named his wife, Violet, as next-of-kin.

His rank was acting sergeant by the time his unit departed for England aboard the SS *Grampian*. The ship arrived in England

October 10, 1917. In December of that year, Acting Sergeant Smeaton reverted to a lower rank—gunner—to expedite his passage to the front lines.

Finally, on April Fool's Day 1918, Smeaton proceeded to France. He was clearly well regarded by his commanders. In May he was promoted to corporal, and in early September to sergeant. By that time, the Canada Corps was immersed in the fierce fighting of what became known as the Last Hundred Days of the war. Shortly after his second promotion and now attached to the 18th Siege Battery, Sergeant Smeaton was awarded the Military Medal for bravery in the field—one of four men featured in this book who earned the award.

Sergeant Smeaton, MM, managed to carry out his duties to King and Country for the remaining weeks of the war without coming to major harm. His medical records indicate no wounds or serious illness.

As was the case for thousands of other Canadian soldiers, the end of the war did not immediately bring about Smeaton's deliverance from soldierly duty. He remained in France until early April 1919, when he was transported to Kinmel Park in North Wales, where Canadians had mutinied in March over the time it was taking to repatriate them to Canada. Between March 4 and 5, five soldiers among the rioters were killed, and another twenty-three wounded.

Two months after the Kinmel insurrection, Smeaton finally shipped out for Canada. He embarked from Southampton aboard HMT *Mauretania* on May 3, arriving six days later in Halifax. Finally, on May 12, 1919, Smeaton was discharged from the CEF. By then he was back in his home on Quebec Street in Outremont, a year and a half after he had last seen his wife.

Smeaton had so impressed the higher-ups of the NHA that upon his return home he was offered a role as a referee with the NHA's successor, the NHL. Smeaton learned not to be intimidated by players, but he found adjusting to fan abuse more challenging, especially when spectators aimed missiles not just at him but also at his wife seated in the Montreal stands.

1930–31 Philadelphia Quakers

He carried out his ice-arbiter duties through to 1930, when he was tempted by a new challenge: the role of head coach with a new NHL franchise, the Philadelphia Quakers.

Smeaton's success as referee did not carry over to his new assignment behind the Quakers bench. In 1930–31, the NHL played a forty-four–game regular schedule. The Philadelphians won precisely four of those games. Four games ended in ties, thirty-six in losses. The Quakers finished dead last in the American Division, twenty-seven points in arrears of the next-worst Detroit Falcons. After coaching for one year, Smeaton resumed his previous referee role with the NHL.

He retired from his on-ice duties in 1937 at age forty-seven but carried on for a time as the league's referee-in-chief. Throughout his NHL career, he managed to successfully balance his on-ice duties with those assigned by the Sun Life people: he was promoted within the company, eventually becoming general manager of its Ottawa and Montreal operations.

Having started out as a player and then become a referee and head coach, Smeaton had one more hockey role to fill. In 1893, when Lord Stanley had donated his silverware as the prize awarded to the country's best amateur hockey club, he appointed trustees. Trustees were the custodians responsible for seeing that the Cup was awarded in accordance with the established rules—and for looking after the bowl's welfare and safekeeping.

In 1946, Smeaton was appointed as Stanley Cup trustee. He served in the capacity for thirty-two years, the majority of them alongside Mervyn "Red" Dutton, the soldier-player who had nearly lost a leg at Vimy Ridge. Cooper Smeaton carried on in his role as trustee until 1978. By that time he had already been a member of the Hockey Hall of Fame—in the Hall's on-ice official division—for seventeen years.

Lauded for his fearlessness, fairness, and integrity, Cooper Smeaton was inducted in the Hockey Hall of Fame in 1961, together with Percy LeSueur and Frank Rankin.

Smeaton lived a long, fruitful life: he died at Montreal in his eighty-ninth year in October 1978. He is buried in Montreal's Mount Royal Cemetery, not far from the final resting place of the man who was his supreme commander in the Last Hundred Days of the Great War: Sir Arthur Currie.

Frank the Flash Foyston

Stanley Cup Magnet

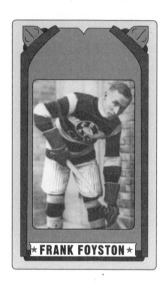

★ FRANK FOYSTON ★

**Toronto Blueshirts/Seattle Metropolitans/
Victoria Cougars/Detroit Cougars** (1912–28)

Canadian Expeditionary Force (1918)

Hockey Hall of Fame (1958)

★ ★ ★

Though many people may never have heard of it, the tiny hamlet of Minesing, Ontario, is a community of some consequence. The village is on the doorstep of the Minesing Wetlands, which extend from Barrie to Georgian Bay and are rated as the biggest and most important fen bog in southern Ontario. In addition to hosting a popular late-winter festival and a Labour Day slo-pitch softball tournament of some renown, Minesing is also celebrated as the birthplace of Hockey Hall-of-Famer Frank Corbett Foyston, a several-time All-Star and Stanley Cup champion with three different pro hockey teams, a luminary widely known in his prime as The Flash.

The Flash was seventeen when he first made a name for himself as a hockey amateur in Barrie. He turned pro in 1912, at age twenty-one, with the Toronto Blueshirts of the NHA, the NHL precursor and principal professional league of its time. Foyston skated three seasons with the Blueshirts and quickly established himself as one of the team's leading lights. He capped his time in Toronto with a Stanley Cup victory in 1914.

Foyston capitalized on his success in Toronto: induced by the prospect of a bigger, better pay cheque, he took his act to Seattle of the Pacific Coast Hockey Association, a league organized by the legendary Patrick brothers—Lester and Frank—whose vast ambitions included the aim of making the PCHA the best and boldest league in all of professional hockey. In his second season on the shores of Puget Sound, Foyston scored thirty-six goals in twenty-four scheduled games, led the Metropolitans to the PCHA title, and then defeated the Montreal Canadiens to take the Stanley Cup, a first for a U.S.-based team.

By 1917, the war had been raging for three years. All of the players introduced in the preceding pages were hockey men who decided that the circumstances of their time warranted their setting aside their skates and sticks to take up arms in defence of King and Country. Frank Foyston was not one of them. He became a soldier in the Canadian Expeditionary Force (CEF) not because he wanted to but because Robert Borden—the prime minister whose image graces Canada's hundred-dollar bill—obliged him to.

The war had by now lost almost all the allure it had seemed to offer young men and boys three years earlier. Given the appalling casualty figures and nightmare accounts of the conditions in which soldiers were fighting and dying in French and Belgian battlefields, recruitment efforts could no longer keep pace with the rapidly accumulating losses. Borden and his Cabinet colleagues had given assurance early in the war that soldiers would be enlisted in the CEF on a strictly voluntary basis. By 1917—the year of Vimy, Hill 70, and, ultimately the worst of them all, Passchendaele—it had become clear that Canada could no longer keep the commitments it had given to Britain without resorting to conscription.

Borden cobbled together a coalition comprising his own Conservative caucus and supportive Liberals. The Unionist coalition pushed through the *Military Service Act*, offending much of the province of Quebec and western farmers, as well as unionists, pacifists, and Canadians of non-British extraction. In the firestorm that ensued, the country nearly broke apart at the seams.

Young men all over Canada were drafted into the CEF whether they were ready or not. One of them was MSA conscript number 2022458, Frank Foyston. The Flash signed his draft document in Vancouver on April 2, 1918.

In the document, he described his "trade or calling" not as *hockey professional* but *rancher*. Under next-of-kin, he listed his father, Alfred Foyston, of Minesing.

By April 1918 there was still plenty enough war remaining that conscripts had time to undergo training and find themselves shipped to France. Many conscripted soldiers did their bit in the last momentous Hundred Days of the war, and many died. The last Canadian to be killed in the war was a conscript, killed by an enemy sniper two minutes before the eleventh hour of the eleventh day of November 1918.

Frank Foyston was not among his fellow conscripts fighting at Cambrai, Valenciennes, and Mons. Less than a month after signing his draft document, he was discharged from the CEF so that he could join the Royal Flying Corps—a better destination, perhaps, for a hockey star nicknamed The Flash.

Neither the war nor the Royal Flying Corps were much of an inconvenience to Foyston. He missed the start of the 1918–19 PCHA regular season but managed to return to Seattle in plenty of time to play eighteen of Seattle's twenty regular-schedule games. He hadn't lost his scoring touch: in those eighteen games, he scored fifteen goals, good enough to rank second in team scoring.

In 1924, now thirty-three years old and with nine seasons behind him in Seattle, Foyston crossed the Strait of Juan de Fuca and took a position as a forward with Lester Patrick's Victoria Cougars. He

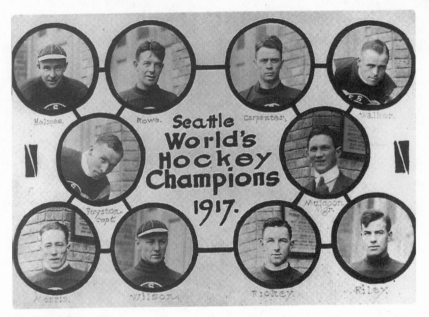

1917 Seattle Metropolitans

had won a Stanley Cup with his first two pro teams and did it again in Victoria. In his first season in the British Columbian capital, Foyston hoisted the Cup for a third time. The Cougars defeated the NHL's Montreal Canadiens three games to one in the Cup playoff. No one knew it back then, but that would be the last time that a team not part of the NHL would see its name inscribed on Lord Stanley's bowl. By 1927 the Stanley Cup would be the exclusive preserve of the NHL.

By 1926 Flash Foyston was an old man by professional hockey standards. At age thirty-five, he became an NHL rookie. He played two final seasons with the Detroit Cougars—a team transplanted from Victoria when the western league folded at the end of the 1926–27 season. The Detroit years were an anomaly in Foyston's career: he did *not* win a Stanley Cup there.

He may not have had a career as a soldier to boast about to the grandchildren, but Frank Foyston could certainly feel proud of his hockey résumé. Over the course of seventeen pro seasons, The Flash

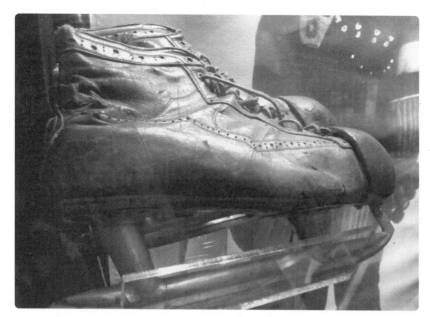

Frank Foyston skates

scored 282 goals in 407 regular-season and playoff games. Three times a Stanley Cup winner, eight times an All-Star, Foyston was inducted in the Hockey Hall of Fame in 1958, one of fourteen former players drafted into the Hall that year. Among the artefacts on display at the Hall of Fame are a pair of the skates in which Foyston flashed to glory in his Seattle years.

Foyston lived long enough to relish the honour. Aged sixty-seven the year of his induction, he would live another eight years before dying at age seventy-five at Seattle in 1966.

Scotty Davidson

Celebrated On and Off the Ice

**Kingston 14th Regiment/Calgary Athletics/
Toronto Blueshirts** (1908–14)

2nd Battalion Canadian Expeditionary Force
(1914–15)

Hockey Hall of Fame (1950)

★ ★ ★

Robert Borden had no need of conscription to entice Allan Davidson into becoming a soldier in the Canadian Expeditionary Force. After leading his Toronto Blueshirts to the NHA title and a Stanley Cup victory in 1914, Davidson was a very early volunteer in the CEF, travelling one month after the war broke out to enlist at Valcartier, Quebec, where Borden's Minister of Militia, Sam Hughes, was building the CEF from the ground up.

Allan Davidson never had a nickname like The Flash. His middle name was McLean and, reflecting his understated Scots Highland heritage, he was simply Scotty to his hockey teammates.

At age seventeen, Davidson was already a hockey luminary. In the 1908–09 season, he played a key role in helping his OHA team, the Kingston 14th Regiment team, claim the OHA championship. One of his teammates on that squad was George Richardson. Richardson, then twenty-two, scored eight goals in the course of the club's four scheduled games. Davidson, five years younger, matched his teammate goal for goal. It would turn out to be the only hockey campaign they shared as on-ice teammates, but Richardson and Davidson would eventually become comrades in an endeavour far more significant than a hockey game.

Allan "Scotty" Davidson/Toronto Blueshirts

After another amateur season, with the Calgary Athletics of the Southern Alberta Senior Hockey (SASH) League in 1911–12, Allan Davidson turned professional in 1912 with the NHA Toronto Blueshirts. The rigours of the pro game didn't slow him a bit. In twenty games, the twenty-one-year-old scored nineteen goals, enough to make him second in team scoring behind another future Hall-of-Famer, Frank Nighbor. Despite the efforts of their scoring leaders, though, the Blueshirts won only nine of their twenty scheduled games and finished fourth in the six-team NHA.

A year of seasoning worked wonders for the Toronto club. In 1913–14, the Blueshirts improved their victory total from nine to thirteen and finished tied for first with the mighty Montreal Canadiens. Leading the way this time for the Blueshirts was Scotty Davidson with twenty-three goals—well ahead of his teammate Flash Foyston's sixteen. Davidson, Foyston, and company beat the Montrealers 6–2 in a two-game total-point series to take the NHA title.

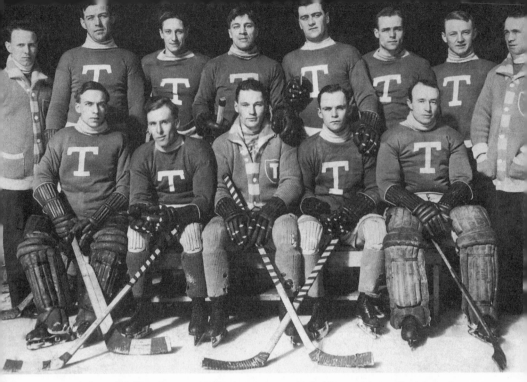

1914 Toronto Blueshirts, front row: **Frank Foyston**, second left; **Allan Davidson**, third left; back row: **George McNamara**, fifth left

With the Stanley Cup up for grabs, the Toronto club then met a challenge from the champions of the PCHA, the Victoria Aristocrats. The legendary Lester Patrick wore three caps for the Aristocrats— owner, coach, and player. Patrick had contributed in every way to the Aristocrats' success in 1913–14, but even with him on board the Victoria club was no match for Toronto: the Blueshirts won the best-of-five series in straight games, outscoring the Victoria squad 13–8. Scotty Davidson was a Stanley Cup champion at age twenty-two.

A careful look at the 1913–14 Blueshirts team photograph reveals a good deal about the era. This is not the collection of skating million-aires one sees in a portrait of latter-day Stanley Cup winners. Some of the players' gear is mismatched, their sticks worn, their leggings threadbare and holed. Davidson, handsome and determined-looking, sits front and centre. Despite his tender years he is the team captain. Foyston, smaller than his captain, sits to Davidson's right but leans a little the other way, as if in deference. Another teammate featured in this book, George McNamara, stands behind Davidson and to his left.

While Foyston would go on to greater hockey glory, the final 2–1 victory over Victoria—March 19, 1914—would be the last game of Davidson's hockey career.

He enlisted for overseas service on September 22, describing his "trade or calling" not as *hockey professional* but *machinist*. Very soon thereafter, on October 3, Davidson shipped out with his unit, the 14th Regiment, for Europe and active service.

Like so many other military units that existed at the outbreak of the war—or were mobilized in its early months—the 14th was not kept intact for service at the Western Front. The men of the 14th were scattered among front-line fighting battalions. Davidson found himself assigned to the 2nd Battalion (Eastern Ontario Regiment)—the same battalion in which George Richardson served.

It was in the 2nd during the fighting in and near the French hamlet of Givenchy that Allan Davidson breathed his last—on June 16, 1915. The death register card is laconic: "Was instantly killed by a shell which exploded near him in the trench."

A note in his service record indicates that Davidson was "killed instantly by a shell falling in the trench. He was practically blown to pieces." The same note indicates that Lance-Corporal Davidson's remains were buried with the bodies of two other 2nd Battalion men killed that day. Which two we can only guess—six men from the battalion died June 16.

A Calgary newspaper item that appeared shortly after Davidson's death delivers a very different account from that of the service record. The piece quotes from a letter written by none other than George Richardson, Davidson's old 14th Regiment teammate in Kingston. "He was absolutely fearless in the face of the greatest danger," Richardson wrote, describing a final scene in which Davidson and others had crawled out to within a few feet of the German line before hurling their grenades into enemy ranks.

In the newspaper account, some of Davidson's companions are said to have retreated before throwing all their grenades, but Davidson remained until his were gone. His body was recovered the following morning "riddled with bullets and jabbed with bayonets."

Was Richardson's dramatic tribute coloured by his legendary loyalty, kindness, and consideration? Was the newspaper account more fanciful and less reliable than the official record? Perhaps.

We can be sure of one thing: in both accounts, Davidson is said to have been buried·in a battlefield grave near the place he fell. Many battlefield graves were destroyed by subsequent military action and such was the case with Davidson's. Today he is remembered—like Frank McGee and more than eleven thousand other Canadian soldiers who died in France and have no known grave—on the Vimy monument.

The Calgary news item opens with speculation that Davidson would likely have been awarded a gallantry decoration had he lived—the Distinguished Conduct Medal, perhaps even the Victoria Cross. It closes with the observation that he was "the best all round player in the National [Hockey] Association." It was a view of Davidson the hockey player that would be underscored a few years later, in 1925, when he was selected by *Maclean's* as the right-winger on the magazine's all-time All-Star team.

Though his career as an elite amateur and professional hockey player ran to a mere sixty-one games of regular-season and playoff games, Scotty Davidson was an early inductee in the Hockey Hall of Fame, a member of the 1950 draft together with Harry Trihey and his fellow casualty of war, George Richardson.

Frank Rankin

Least Famed of Them All?

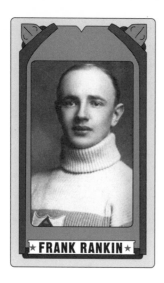

**Toronto Eaton's/
Toronto St. Michael's** (1910–14)

**No. 2 Artillery Depot,
Canadian Expeditionary Force** (1918)

Hockey Hall of Fame (1961)

★ ★ ★

If the players enshrined in the Hockey Hall of Fame were to be ranked according to the degree of their fame, who would stand first among them? Gordie Howe? Bobby Orr? Wayne Gretzky? If these three are among the most famed of famous hockey players, it might be that the Hall member at the other end of the spectrum would be a fellow inducted in 1961 together with Maurice "The Rocket" Richard: Frank Gilchrist Rankin. It may be that even among hockey history aficionados, none of the 271 players in the Hall has been quite so forgotten as Rankin.

Frank Rankin stood all of five feet, five inches tall and weighed 145 pounds in the prime of his playing career—about four inches and forty pounds slighter than the smallest player in today's NHL. Rankin's career took flight when he was thirteen years old in the junior amateur ranks at Stratford, Ontario—a hockey hotbed at the time. He played six seasons of junior amateur hockey at Stratford before graduating to the senior ranks of the OHA at age nineteen in 1910. In the days of seven-man hockey, Rankin played rover, a position that began to disappear in 1910 and would be entirely gone from hockey by 1923.

In the 1910–11 season, playing rover for the Toronto Eaton's club of the OHA, Rankin scored an impressive fifteen goals in just four regular-schedule games for the Eaton's lads and then added four more in two playoff games. That made him a first-team OHA All-Star. Although not quite as prolific the following season—six goals in six games—Rankin was still an exceptional enough scorer to make the OHA second All-Star team.

In 1912–13, rover Rankin took his game across town to another OHA club, Toronto St. Michael's, where he shone more brightly than ever, scoring twenty-two times in just five regular-schedule games—an average of more than four goals a game. Once again he was a first-team All-Star. The following year, he scored ten goals in the two games he played for St. Michael's—a rate of *five* per game.

Then, at the grand old age of twenty-two in 1914, Rankin's playing days were over. The year is not telling. In contrast to Frank McGee, George Richardson, and Scotty Davidson, Rankin's hockey career was *not* derailed by war. We do not know why Rankin quit the game at such a young age but the war was not to blame: in 1914 Rankin did not swap his hockey sweater for the tunic of a Canadian soldier.

Like the better-known and more prolific Frank Foyston, Rankin did not become a soldier until Prime Minister Robert Borden gave him no choice in the matter. Rankin is qualified for inclusion in the list of Hockey Hall of Fame players who were also soldiers of the Great War only by the narrowest of margins: he completed his attestation under the

Military Service Act just nine days before the end of the war—November 2, 1918—and thus avoided the fate that befell CEF volunteers McGee, Davidson, and Richardson.

But other circumstances would give Frank Rankin an opportunity to serve Canada on a world stage of a different sort.

By 1922—eight years after the end of his playing days—Rankin was still in hockey. At age thirty-one, in his new role as coach of the Toronto Granites of the OHA senior division, he appeared to be just as effective as he had been on the ice a decade earlier. The preceding season, 1921–22, the Granites had been coached by a man named Frank Carroll whose résumé included stints as a trainer with the 1914 Toronto Blueshirts and the 1917 228th Battalion Northern Fusiliers. Carroll was effective, coaching the Granites to a 7–3 record, the OHA senior title, and an Allan Cup—the Canadian amateur championship—victory.

Despite Carroll's success, Frank Rankin took over as coach for the 1922–23 season. The Granites improved their regular-season record to nine victories in twelve games. That matched the record of the rival Hamilton Tigers, but the Granites took the OHA title by outscoring the Tigers 6–4 in a two-game playoff. Rankin's Granites then proceeded to

1924 Canadian Hockey Olympians

dominate the University of Saskatchewan 11–2 to secure the Allan Cup for a second straight year.

On the strength of that victory, the Granites qualified themselves to represent Canada at the 1924 Olympic Games in Chamonix, France. In modern times, Canada has been a powerhouse in Olympic hockey— Canadians have won three of the last four hockey gold medals—but winning the gold is nothing like a sure bet in the modern game. In 1924, it was a very different matter.

Rankin was celebrated for his coaching at the Chamonix games, but it is easy to imagine that Frank Carroll or another coach might have been equally successful. In the round-robin portion of the tournament the Canadians beat Sweden 22–0. That was the Canadians' tightest score in the round-robin: Czechoslovakia fell 30–0 in the second game and then it was the turn of the Swiss to face the Canadian juggernaut. Switzerland lost 33–0, a scoring hurricane of better than a goal every two minutes. It could not have been a joy being the man in the Swiss goal.

The gold medal game was closer. As would be the case in the 2002 Olympics and again in 2010, the gold medal game in 1924 pitted Canada against the United States. Canada won 6–1, a closer result than in any of the round-robin games but a decisive one nonetheless.

In his whole career, Frank Rankin played a mere thirty-one games of elite senior amateur hockey. He was offered a sack of money to turn professional but never did. As a player he won neither a Stanley Cup nor an Allan Cup, but in 1961, his career seventy-one goals in just thirty-one games were enough to persuade electors to place him in the Hockey Hall of Fame. There were eleven players in the 1961 draft. They included Rocket Richard—who scored 626 goals in more than eleven hundred NHL regular-season and playoff games—and Percy LeSueur.

It might have been a pleasant surprise for the 1924 Olympic champion coach had he been around to hear of the honour, but Rankin had been gone nearly thirty years by that time. He died where he had first starred as a hockey player, at Stratford, in the summer of 1932. The cause of death was blood poisoning. He was only forty-one.

Gardiner, Gretzky,
and Nobody Else

★ H. GARDINER ★

2nd Canadian Mounted Rifles (1915–18)

**Calgary Tigers/Montreal Canadiens/
Chicago Blackhawks** (1921–29)

Hockey Hall of Fame (1958)

★ ★ ★

Herb Gardiner started making a name for himself in Winnipeg amateur hockey circles at the age of fifteen in 1906. He skated for a succession of now mostly forgotten Winnipeg clubs—Merchants Bank, Victorias, and Northern Crowns—before winding up his amateur days two provinces west with the Monarchs of the Calgary City League in 1914–15. The league schedule was a limited one—each of three teams played only four games. The Monarchs lost all four of theirs.

Whether Gardiner played all four Monarchs games isn't clear from the surviving hockey records, but it seems that events beyond the control of the Calgary City League (CCL) may have interrupted Herb's time in

Calgary. Soon after the outbreak of war, Gardiner set his hockey gear aside and became an early volunteer with the Canadian Expeditionary Force. He enlisted in his home town, Winnipeg, on January 4, 1915. In the autumn of that year, Herbert Martin Gardiner found himself on the other side of the Atlantic, serving with an infantry battalion, the 2nd Canadian Mounted Rifles.

He had been a bank employee in his early working days—hence his service with the 1908 Merchants Bank hockey club back in 1908—but by 1915, he had qualified as a land surveyor and it was by that "trade or calling" that he identified himself in his attestation document.

Gardiner's war service record, a longish one at more than a hundred pages, reveals a good deal about his days in uniform. It is clear from the record that he enjoyed considerable success as a soldier. He was promoted several times—from private, to corporal, to sergeant, and ultimately to lieutenant.

Despite those promotions, it is equally clear from his service record that military life was not always smooth sailing for him. In early June 1916—perhaps as a consequence of his battalion's role in the Battle of Mount Sorrel—he was a casualty, having received a gunshot wound to the nose. There followed a string of other hospital stays—for jaundice, pleurisy, and other respiratory ailments.

One of the attending military doctors noted something about Lieutenant Gardiner that was not at all rare among soldiers of the Great War but was certainly ill-advised for a man suffering from a string of breathing issues: he was a heavy smoker. The upshot of the ongoing medical problems was that Gardiner was invalided back to Canada in March 1918. Herb Gardiner's war was over, but before being discharged he assigned his soldier's separation allowance to his widowed mother in Winnipeg.

After the war the Gardiner resumed working for the Canadian Pacific Railway as a surveyor. He played a little amateur hockey on the side—first for the Calgary Rotarians, 1918–19, and then the Wanderers for a couple of seasons, '19–21. By 1921 he was thirty years old. A late bloomer if there ever was one, Gardiner decided to become a hockey professional. He joined the Calgary Tigers of the Western Canada Hockey League (WCHL), a circuit that could make a legitimate claim to being the equal of the NHL.

Over the course of the next five years, heavy smoker or not, Herb Gardiner became a top-flight pro hockey player. In 1923, and again in 1925, he was a first-team WCHL All-Star defenceman, a teammate of another future Hall-of-Famer whose story appears in this book, Mervyn "Red" Dutton.

A measure of the distance Herb Gardiner had travelled from relative anonymity in the Winnipeg bankers league to pro hockey All-Star was this: he found himself featured on a hockey card. In 1923, a candy manufacturer, Paulin's of Winnipeg, introduced a seventy-card series called Famous Hockey Players, which featured luminaries of the WCHL. The back of each card invited boys, once they had put together a complete set, to mail it to Paulin's for a free hockey stick and the return of their cards. For female collectors, Paulin's had an alternative offer: "Girls, if you don't want a Hockey Stick, you may choose a box of Paulin's Delicious Chocolates." Herb Gardiner's card was number 63 in the series.

In 1924, Gardiner, Dutton, and their fellow Calgary Tigers defeated the Regina Capitals in a two-game playoff to earn the WCHL title. The Calgarians then took on the mighty Montreal Canadiens of the NHL for the Stanley Cup. Gardiner and his teammates lost that challenge in two straight games, but someone in Montreal management must have liked what he had seen of the Calgary defenceman.

Gardiner played one more year in Calgary, 1925–26, and then something quite out of the ordinary unfolded. On October 20, 1926, he was traded to none other than the Montreal Canadiens, not for a disposable Canadiens player but for cash. On that momentous day Herb Gardiner was aged thirty-five years, five months, and twelve days. He was also now an NHL rookie.

It was remarkable enough to become a first-year player in the premier professional league at the age of thirty-five, but Herb Gardiner had another, even more noteworthy trick up his sleeve. He flourished behind the blue line for the Canadiens. He played all forty-four games of the regular schedule, then four more in the playoffs. The Canadiens had finished dead last in the NHL the previous season, winning only eleven of thirty-six regular-schedule games. With Herb Gardiner on board, the Montrealers were transformed, winning twenty-eight games in a forty-four–game schedule, placing them second best in the Canadian Division. The Canadiens fell to the eventual league-champion Ottawa Senators in the NHL playoffs, but then Gardiner accomplished the most extraordinary thing of all: the thirty-five-year-old rookie was voted the NHL's Most Valuable Player for the 1926–27 season.

How many times has a rookie won the Hart Trophy as an NHL MVP? The answer is *two*. Herb Gardiner was the first in 1927. The second was Wayne Gretzky in 1980.

Herb Gardiner/
Montreal Canadiens.
1960–61 Topps
All-Time Greats

There was nothing Herb Gardiner could possibly do to surpass himself. He played another full forty-four–game schedule with Montreal in 1927–28 before being loaned to the Chicago Blackhawks as playing coach in '28–29. However, his time in Chicago was less glorious than his rookie year had been in Montreal. The Hawks finished last in the American Division, and Gardiner went back to Montreal for a seven-game swan song as a Canadiens player. Finally, at age thirty-eight, his playing days were over.

Late bloomer in hockey, wounded veteran of the Great War, most valuable player as a thirty-five-year-old NHL rookie, Gardiner was inducted in the Hockey Hall of Fame in 1958, part of a draft that included eleven players who had done their bit for Canada in the Great War.

Herb Gardiner had a few years to enjoy the tribute paid to him. He died in his eighty-first year, in Philadelphia in January 1972.

3

SECOND PERIOD

Hobey Baker

The Man Who Had It All

★ HOBEY BAKER ★

**Princeton University Tigers/
New York St. Nicholas** (1910–16)

**U.S. Air Force 103rd, 13th,
and 141st Aero Squadrons** (1917–18)

Hockey Hall of Fame (1945)

★ ★ ★

Hobey Baker had it all—he was a star athlete in multiple sports; an academic success at an esteemed Ivy League university; the focus of admiration, even adulation, from much of his university community and far beyond; and a wartime turn as a fighter pilot in a U.S. air squadron with a storied pedigree.

The scion of a prominent Philadelphia family, the teenaged Hobart Amory Hare Baker was sent to a top-drawer preparatory school, St. Paul's in Concord, New Hampshire. It was there that he was introduced to hockey, which he quickly mastered. By the age of fifteen, young Hobart was a star not just of the school's hockey and football teams but in several other sports too—baseball, swimming, golf, and track, just for starters.

He entered Princeton University at age eighteen in 1908. He could have outshone his fellows in any number of the university's athletic programs but the school's rules barred students from playing more than two varsity sports. After a brief baseball distraction, Baker chose hockey and football. Over the course of his four years at Princeton he led his Tigers to three national championships—one in football, two in hockey.

He captained the Tigers to the Ivy League hockey title in 1912 and in 1914. In the 1913–14 season, his senior year, he scored twelve goals in Princeton's eleven games. Comprehensive scoring statistics were not kept at the time, but Emil Salvini, a Baker biographer, believed that he might have scored more than a hundred goals for the Tigers over his four-year span in New Jersey.

Baker was renowned not only for his skill and talent on the ice but also for his gentlemanly conduct. Those paying close attention during his Princeton years claimed that he was assessed only a single minor penalty in four years—a career total of just two minutes in the penalty box.

Magnificent as it was, Baker's university hockey résumé might have been one accomplishment better. At the end of February 1914, the Tigers travelled to Ottawa to play a single game at Dey's Arena to decide the North American intercollegiate championship. Unhappily for the Princeton skaters, they lost by a single goal, 3–2, to their Canadian opponents from the University of Ottawa.

After Princeton, Baker played two seasons with the New York St. Nicholas club of the American Amateur Hockey League (AAHL). There he continued to shine brightly, scoring twenty-six goals in fifteen games between 1914 and 1916.

After graduating in 1914, he worked for the J.P. Morgan Bank, a situation he clearly felt was less glamorous than the role of cherished and admired hockey and football player. In 1916, he found something more enticing to take up as a sideline: he joined a civilian flight corps and learned to fly.

The United States entered the war in April 1917. Baker left for Europe in the summer of that same year, in one of the first U.S. contingents to go overseas. Eager to get into action as quickly as he could, he was frustrated by bureaucratic delays, including a requirement to satisfy a French certification procedure that obliged him, among his other duties, to become proficient in the language.

More aggravations arose. He had to travel to England for further training. Another wait resulted from the requirement that he teach other U.S. fliers what he had learned in England. Then, finally, in April 1918—after nearly a year in Europe without having seen any action—Baker was sent to the front. His initial unit was the 103rd Aero Squadron, a formation established earlier in 1918 that comprised U.S. airmen who had originally served with the famed Lafayette Escadrille and Lafayette Flying Corps.

The following month, Airman Baker helped bring down his first enemy flier. Despite all the excitement he had savoured as a Princeton hockey and football star, Baker described this event as the biggest thrill of his life. On the strength of his first confirmed "kill," Baker was awarded a Croix de Guerre by the French government.

Much admired as an athlete, he attracted attention as an aviator too. The commander of the 13th Aero Squadron wanted Baker for the role of flight commander in his squadron. The commander got his way: Baker transferred to the 13th. Two more victories followed. Then, in August 1918, the former Princeton star was given command of his own unit, the 141st Aero Squadron: 26 pilots and 180 enlisted men. Delays in the provision of aircraft and equipment led to further aggravation for Squadron Leader Baker. Before the problems were resolved, the war came to a close. There would be no more thrilling victories over enemy fliers in the skies above the Western Front. With a total of three credited kills, he fell two short of the number—five—required for recognition as a First World War fighter ace.

In the month following the November 11 Armistice, Baker received orders to return to the United States. He was far from happy about it. Scarce though his triumphs in the air had been, Baker had loved his time as a wartime fighter pilot. He chafed that his opportunities for glory in the air were gone and fretted that civilian life back in his homeland couldn't possibly measure up to the excitement he had savoured in the last months of the war.

Before departing the 141st airbase at Toul, France, Baker decided he absolutely had to take one last flight out of his squadron's airfield. Rather than using his own SPAD *S XIII*, Baker took to the air in heavy rain in another SPAD that had just undergone repairs. The SPAD's engine failed just a quarter mile into the flight, and the aircraft crashed nose-first a few hundred yards from the Toul airfield. Baker died of his injuries within minutes of the crash. He was twenty-six.

Hobey Baker had made it plain that, for him, the war's end offered only bleak prospects: he was not cut out for a boring civilian life. Nothing he could foresee offered anything like the thrills he had relished as a star athlete or Croix de Guerre–decorated fighter pilot. Was the crash an accident? More than a few people wondered.

Spad *S.XIII*

Baker's death caused consternation among those who had known, admired, and loved him. In addition to all his other assets, he was uncommonly charismatic and good-looking. One of his more famous admirers was the American novelist F. Scott Fitzgerald. Fitzgerald's first novel, *This Side of Paradise* (1920), features a character inspired by the irresistible Hobey Baker.

In 1945, Hobey Baker was among the first eleven players inducted in the Hockey Hall of Fame. Included in that inaugural group was another casualty of war, the great Frank McGee. In 1921, Princeton opened a new hockey arena—the Hobey Baker Memorial Rink. In 1981, an annual award was established to honour the U.S. collegiate hockey player judged to be best in all the land—the Hobey Baker Award.

In addition to his place in the Hockey Hall of Fame, Baker was inducted in the U.S. College Football Hall of Fame in 1975.

He is the only man enshrined in both institutions.

Punch Broadbent

Gadabout, Bombardier, Goal-Scorer

★ H. BROADBENT ★

**Ottawa Senators/
Montreal Maroons/
New York Americans** (1912–29)

**6th Brigade/7th Brigade,
Canadian Field Artillery** (1915–19)

Hockey Hall of Fame (1962)

★ ★ ★

The pride of the nation's capital, Harry Lawton "Punch" Broadbent commenced a stellar hockey career as a sixteen-year-old amateur in 1908. Over the ensuing four hockey seasons, he delivered his skills for a string of now mostly forgotten Ottawa teams—the Emmets, Seconds, Cliffsides, New Edinburghs, and Hull Volants—a list demonstrating not just that young Harry was a hockey will-o'-the-wisp but that the naming of hockey teams may be a lost art.

In 1912, Broadbent decided that playing hockey for the pure joy of the game might be further enhanced if he could do it for profit at the same time. He became a hockey pro—and didn't have to leave town to do it. At age twenty he joined the Ottawa Senators, an organization that by that time was already a storied hockey institution. Founded in 1893, the Senators had been a strictly amateur club for the first eleven years of its existence. They were several-time victors in a string of Stanley Cup challenges.

Over the course of its first incarnation—before being revived as a National Hockey League (NHL) expansion team in 1992—the Senators would win the Stanley Cup eleven times—but never again after 1927.

As a Senators rookie in 1912–13, Broadbent did very nicely, scoring twenty goals in the same number of scheduled Senators games. That season was the Senators' fourth in the National Hockey Association (NHA), which was considered the premier professional league of its time. Harry's twenty goals, while impressive, were not enough to get his club into the NHA post-season that year: the '12–13 Senators finished fifth, out of the playoffs.

Broadbent's production took a dip the following season—eight goals in seventeen games—but in his third NHA season, 1914–15, at age twenty-two, he gleamed brighter than ever, scoring twenty-four times in his club's twenty games, more than double that achieved by the team's next-best scorer. In that season he also recorded a career high in penalty minutes—115 of them. That figure was also more than double the number earned by the next-most-penalized Senator: Broadbent was not only a goal-scorer but clearly a bruiser too.

The 1914–15 Ottawa team finished the regular season tied with the Montreal Wanderers for the best record in the NHA: fourteen victories in twenty games. Ottawa won the NHA playoff and then faced off against the Vancouver Millionaires of the Pacific Coast Hockey Association (PCHA). The Vancouver team provided ample evidence to justify its boosters' claim that the PCHA was the equal of the NHA: the Millionaires won the best-of-five final series in straight games, outscoring Punch Broadbent and his Ottawa collaborators by an aggregate 26–8 score. It was the first Stanley Cup victory for a west coast team.

The 1914–15 Senators game sweater was different from the norm: it featured crossed flags—the Canadian red ensign and the Union Jack—to acknowledge that Canada and Britain were now nations at war.

In the prime of his hockey career, Broadbent might have followed the lead of Frank Foyston and other hockey stalwarts and decided to let others answer the call of duty from King and Country. Instead, he enlisted in the Canadian Expeditionary Force (CEF) in the summer of 1915, listing his "trade or calling" not as *hockey professional* but *clerk*. He named his mother as next-of-kin.

In Broadbent's early days as a CEF soldier, his progress to the front lines was delayed by a stint in hospital for treatment of a condition not at all rare among CEF men: he had gonorrhea, a condition said by informed observers to be more prevalent in the Canada Corps than in any other of His Majesty's forces.

Other elements of Broadbent's war record were more salubrious than his early medical history. While serving in the Canadian Field Artillery (CFA), Harry was promoted to bombardier in October 1916. In March 1918, he was awarded a Military Medal for bravery in the field—making Bombardier Broadbent one of the small number of hockey player-soldiers in the Hall of Fame awarded a gallantry medal for their heroics in battle.

A subsequent file item indicates that in September 1918 he was sent to England as a candidate for an officer's commission in the CFA. Despite the inauspicious start, Broadbent had done well as a soldier. And he had survived. In January 1919, he returned to Canada on the White Star liner *Olympic*, sister ship of the ill-fated *Titanic*.

Broadbent had lost more than three of his prime hockey years due to the war, but in 1919 he picked up where he had left off and rejoined the Ottawa Senators. By this time the NHA was defunct, with Ottawa now a charter member of the NHL, which had been established in 1917 when Broadbent was away fighting in Europe. He played eight games at the end of the 1918–19 season and then a full schedule the following year. In that full season, Broadbent scored nineteen goals in twenty-one games.

The 1919–20 campaign was a golden year not just for Punch Broadbent but for the entire Senators organization. Ottawa topped the NHL standings with a 19–5 record and won the NHL championship. Then they went one better, defeating the PCHA Seattle Metropolitans for the Stanley Cup. Punch was a Cup winner for the first time. The Senators did it again in '20–21, when Ottawa won the Cup against the team that had vanquished Ottawa back in 1915—the Vancouver Millionaires.

The following season, 1921–22, Broadbent was clearly better than ever at age twenty-nine. That season he scored thirty-two times in twenty-four games, leading Ottawa to a league-best fourteen victories. By this time he was not just his team's most prolific scorer but also the best in the entire NHL. Unfortunately, his personal success did not translate into a Stanley Cup victory. Ottawa lost the NHL title to the Toronto St. Patricks, who went on to beat Vancouver in the Cup final.

But the Senators came back again the following season, 1922–23, winning the NHL title and the Stanley Cup, defeating first Vancouver and then the Edmonton Eskimos of the Western Canada Hockey League (WCHL). The leading scorer in the Cup playoffs was none other than Punch Broadbent, with six goals in as many Cup playoff games.

Now in his thirties, Broadbent would play one more year in Ottawa. In 1924, he was shipped to Montreal, where he played three seasons with the NHL Maroons. Punch scored fourteen and twelve goals in his first two Maroons seasons, respectable numbers but not in the same class as his glory years with the Senators. There *was* a highlight in Montreal, though: one more Stanley Cup victory, in 1926, over the Western Hockey League Victoria Cougars.

It was an historic playoff—the last time that a team not part of the NHL competed for the Stanley Cup and the last season of the western league. From this point forward the Stanley Cup would become an exclusive NHL chattel.

Punch Broadbent's hockey career took two more turns. In 1927, he was traded back to Ottawa. He played forty-three of the Senators' forty-four regular-schedule games in 1927–28, but at age thirty-five, it was clear that the explosive scoring touch that had earned him the nickname Punch had deserted him: he scored only three goals that season.

In October 1928, he was traded one final time—to the New York Americans. In the Big Apple, he scored just once in forty-four games. His career was done.

Harry "Punch" Broadbent was inducted in the Hockey Hall of Fame in 1962. The 1962 class of inductees included eight players featured in this book: all of whom had excelled as hockey players and had also served as soldiers in the Great War.

In contrast to several Hall members who would never know of the honour bestowed upon them, Punch Broadbent could relish the tribute while he still breathed. He died in his eighty-first year in the city of his birth, the place he had performed gloriously for so many years—Ottawa.

Dick Irvin

Player and Coach Extraordinaire

★ DICK IRVIN ★

Portland Rosebuds/
Regina Victorias/
Regina Capitals/
Chicago Blackhawks (1916–29)

Canadian Corps Reinforcement Camp (1918)

Hockey Hall of Fame (1958)

★ ★ ★

A native of Hamilton, Ontario, James Dickinson (Dick) Irvin first made his mark as a hockey player more than twelve hundred miles to the northwest in the hockey hotbed of Winnipeg. Starting at age seventeen in 1908, he played amateur hockey with the junior Strathconas club before moving up to the Strathconas seniors in 1912–13. That year, he scored thirty-two goals in just seven games with the Strathconas. He eventually took his skills to the Winnipeg Monarchs, and in 1916, he led that squad to the Canadian amateur championship—and an Allan Cup.

The following winter, 1916–17, Irvin decided to follow a growing trend: he turned professional. His adjustment to pro hockey proved seamless. With the Portland Rosebuds of the PCHA—imagine a pro hockey team calling itself the Rosebuds today—he notched thirty-five goals in twenty-three games, fourth best in the PCHA.

Despite the success in Portland, Irvin was back playing senior amateur hockey in Winnipeg the next year. Evidently inspired by patriotic zeal and a desire to honour the Canadians fighting in Flanders and France, league organizers gave the Winnipeg clubs names reflecting the great battles Canadians had fought in the war to date: the Winnipeg Somme, Winnipeg Vimy, and Irvin's squad, the Winnipeg Ypres.

Rather than volunteering for service in the Canadian Expeditionary Force, Irvin had spent the war years playing hockey. Finally, in the spring of 1918 at age twenty-six, he lost the option of staying out of the Canadian Expeditionary Force (CEF). In April he was conscripted under provisions of the *Military Service Act*.

In his attestation, he might have given his "trade or calling" as *hockey player* but this was a time when no player, amateur or professional, could make ends meet through the proceeds of hockey alone: Irvin listed his trade as *salesman and butcher*.

Conscript Irvin was lucky: he was able to discharge the duties forced upon him entirely in Canada. The war ended before he was obliged to join other conscripts in the fierce fighting that left many conscripted men casualties in what became known as the war's Last Hundred Days.

Conscription proved deadly for many men forced into the CEF, but it turned out to be only a minor nuisance for Irvin. In 1917–18, he scored a remarkable twenty-nine goals in just eight games with the Winnipeg Ypres. The '18–19 season would turn out to be the only one he would have to sacrifice because of his war obligations. The next year, '19–20, the war was no longer a hindrance, and Irvin scored thirty-two goals in just a dozen games with the Regina Victorias of the Saskatchewan Senior Hockey League.

After another successful year as an amateur, Irvin returned to the pro ranks. In 1921–22, now aged twenty-nine, he went to work for the Regina Capitals of the WCHL, a circuit that could lay legitimate claim to being every bit the equal of the NHL.

In his first season with the Capitals, Irvin demonstrated that he hadn't lost a step on the eve of his thirties: he scored twenty-one goals in the twenty-game regular schedule. His contributions were instrumental in helping the Capitals claim the WCHL title and a berth in the Stanley Cup semi-final against the Vancouver Millionaires of the Pacific Coast league. Irvin's Capitals narrowly won the first game of a two-game, total-point series but were shut out 4–0 in the second, dashing Regina's Cup hopes.

In 1923, Irvin made the big time: he was featured as one of the Famous Hockey Players in the Paulin's hockey card series.

He played three more seasons with the Capitals, scoring as many as fifteen goals in those campaigns—respectable seasons but none of them as impressive as his first year in the WCHL. Then, in 1926, the Capitals' owner stuck a knife in the hearts of Regina fans: he sold the club to businessmen in Portland, Oregon. While fans back in Regina might have been devastated at the betrayal, Dick Irvin was born again. At age thirty-three, he enjoyed a season for the ages with the latest incarnation of his first pro team. Irvin scored thirty-one goals in thirty games for the Rosebuds, second best among league scorers.

The 1925–26 season turned out to be the swan song of what had started out as the PCHA. Organized by the ambitious, innovative Patrick brothers—Lester and Frank—the PCHA had merged with the WCHL in 1924. Throughout its history, the Patricks' league had made a strong case that its brand was as good as any professional hockey played in Canada. In 1926, the league was disbanded.

Deprived of the possibility of further glory in the Rose City, Irvin agreed on terms with a new club in the NHL, the Chicago Blackhawks. At age thirty-four, Irvin was an NHL rookie. Appointed Blackhawks captain, he led the way in scoring, with eighteen goals and eighteen assists in forty-three games—second best among the marksmen in the NHL's American Division.

Two more years as a Blackhawks player followed, but Irvin's best playing days were behind him. In 1928–29, the former Rosebud managed to score just six goals in thirty-nine games. His player career was over at age thirty-six.

However, this opened a door for Dick Irvin to a new vocation at least as celebrated as his playing career: Irvin became a coach. He was appointed Chicago coach for the 1930–31 season. The Blackhawks had a so-so year with Irvin in charge, earning forty-seven points in a forty-eight-game schedule, but he had sufficiently impressed the owner of the Toronto Maple Leafs, Conn Smythe, to be offered the chance to take over as Leafs coach from Art Duncan—a twice-decorated Canadian war hero and fighter pilot ace of the Great War.

In 1931–32, Irvin's first season as Toronto coach, the Leafs finished the regular season two wins in arrears of the Montreal Canadiens, but in the post-season the Leafs beat the coach's former club, Chicago, in the first round, and then vanquished Montreal in the second. In the playoff final—with the Stanley Cup the ultimate reward—Toronto swept the New York Rangers in straight games. For the first time in his hockey life, Dick Irvin was a Stanley Cup champion.

Irvin would guide Toronto to another six Stanley Cup finals as coach, but he never duplicated the first Cup win he accomplished. He departed Toronto in 1940 and was hired by Montreal to revive a Canadiens organization that had fallen on hard times. Montreal had finished dead last in 1939–40—just ten victories in forty-eight games—and was losing fan interest.

It took a while, but Montreal's fortunes did take a turn for the better. Under Irvin's stewardship, the Montrealers improved their victory total over the next four years—from ten to sixteen to eighteen, and finally to nineteen in 1942–43. Then, in 1943, with Maurice Richard leading the way on the ice, Irvin's Canadiens shot to thirty-eight victories in a forty-eight-game schedule. In the final—against Chicago—Montreal prevailed in four straight games. The former Rosebud was a second-time Stanley Cup winner.

He would do it twice more in Montreal—in 1946 and 1953—before surrendering the coaching reins to a man who would enjoy even greater success as Canadiens coach: Toe Blake.

Not quite ready to call an end to his hockey career, Irvin returned to Chicago to coach the Blackhawks for one last season. His encore in Chicago was not what he would have wanted: the Blackhawks won just nineteen times in a schedule now seventy games long—well out of the playoff picture. Now in his sixty-fourth year and suffering from cancer, Dick Irvin called it quits.

He was inducted in the Hockey Hall of Fame in 1958, one of eleven men featured in this book who were both hockey stars and soldiers of the Great War. He could just as easily have been enshrined as a coach, but it is as a player that Dick Irvin is honoured with a Hockey Hall of Fame tablet.

Irvin never knew of the honour given him, as he had been felled by cancer the preceding year. He died at age sixty-four in Montreal, the city electrified by three Stanley Cups achieved by les Glorieux under the guidance of Dick Irvin.

Adventures of
Bullet Joe Simpson

★ JOE SIMPSON ★

**Selkirk Fishermen/Edmonton Eskimos/
New York Americans** (1913–31)

**31st Battalion/61st Battalion/
43rd Battalion, Canadian Expeditionary
Force** (1915–19)

Hockey Hall of Fame (1962)

★ ★ ★

Situated on the Red River not far from its mouth at the southern extremity of Lake Winnipeg, Selkirk, Manitoba, has a present-day population of about ten thousand. The city is home to the Selkirk Steelers of the Manitoba Junior Hockey League, and given the prevalence of ice for a good portion of the year in this part of Canada, it is perhaps no surprise that many of Selkirk's most famous sons are hockey players. The most famous of them all—the only one with a place in the Hockey Hall of Fame—is Harold Edward "Bullet Joe" Simpson.

While still a teenager, Simpson began his career in amateur hockey as Dick Irvin's teammate with the 1912–13 Winnipeg Strathconas. During the next two years, he would also play for the Selkirk Fishermen ('13–14) and Winnipeg Victorias ('14–15).

On August 26, 1915, a few days past his twenty-second birthday, Simpson enlisted in Winnipeg in the 31st Infantry Battalion. He gave his "trade or calling" as *seaman* and his next-of-kin his father, Joseph, back in Selkirk.

Before departing Canada for the Western Front, Simpson played another season of amateur hockey, this time for a squad with a distinctly military bearing, the 61st Battalion. As it turned out, the 61st would not endure as a battalion that reached the war zone intact, but it did make a significant impact as a hockey team.

In the 1915–16 post-season, the 61st Battalion players vanquished first the Winnipeg Monarchs and then Simpson's former club, the Victorias, before facing off against a team from Fort William, Ontario. Simpson and company narrowly defeated their northern Ontario foes, thus qualifying them to play one more series for the Canadian amateur championship. Their adversaries in that final series, the Regina

61st Battalion Hockey Team, **Joe Simpson**, third left, seated

Victorias, were no match for the Winnipeggers: the 61st team outscored Regina 13–3 in a two-game series to take possession of the Allan Cup.

In an evocative team portrait, with the Allan Cup front and centre, Simpson sits with his teammates. They are hockey players and soldiers too. Two of them would be killed in action during the war—one at Hill 70, another at Passchendaele.

Just two weeks after their Allan Cup victory, Simpson and his teammates were on their way to war. Departing from Halifax, they crossed the Atlantic aboard the SS *Olympic* and landed in England in early April.

In several ways, Simpson's war service resembles Punch Broadbent's: a roller-coaster ride of highs and lows.

In August 1916, just a few months after arriving in England, a medical note in Simpson's service record indicates that the young soldier shared an affliction with Broadbent and thousands of other Canadian soldiers: he needed treatment for gonorrhea. He was treated for his condition at Cherry Hinton Military Hospital, Cambridge.

Before the end of the month, Simpson was discharged and returned to his battalion—just in time to be wounded in the Battle of the Somme. His wounds—bullet wounds to the left leg and back—were serious enough to warrant a "blighty": evacuation to a soldiers' hospital in England, this time in Northamptonshire.

In July 1917, Simpson was promoted to lieutenant. The next month, another creditable event is noted in his service record: just like Punch Broadbent, he was awarded a Military Medal, for gallantry.

The service record also includes a noteworthy entry dated February 28, 1918. Simpson is shown as having been dismissed from His Majesty's Service by finding of General Court Martial. No details are recorded, but whatever the offence was, it must not have been heinous—just five days later he was back in King George's service.

In August 1918, early in the Last Hundred Days of the war, Lieutenant Simpson was once again a casualty of war. This time he received a gunshot wound to the right shoulder. It too was a blighty— serious enough to require hospitalization in England, this time in Bristol.

In a note dated October 28, two weeks before the Armistice, a military doctor indicates that Simpson "has been found. . .free from Vermin, Venereal or Infectious Diseases," ready for discharge from hospital. But he was not discharged until early November, just as the war was drawing to a close.

Simpson returned to Manitoba in time to play four games with his former club, the Selkirk Fishermen, at the end of the 1918–19 season as well as a full schedule in '19–20. His war wounds seemed not to be an impediment: he scored nineteen goals in just ten scheduled games for Selkirk.

In 1921, he turned professional with the Edmonton Eskimos of the WCHL. In his first season in the Alberta capital, he scored twenty-one times in twenty-five games and earned himself a spot on the league's first All-Star team. One of his teammates was Gordon "Duke" Keats, another veteran of the Great War featured in this book.

Simpson was again an All-Star the following season, 1922–23.

Joe Simpson/Coach, New York Americans

This time the Eskimos won both the WCHL title and an opportunity to play for the Stanley Cup. Edmonton's opponents in the 1923 Cup final were the NHL Ottawa Senators, led by none other than Punch Broadbent. In the best-of-three series, played at Vancouver's Denman Street Arena, Ottawa won the first game 2–1. In the second game, March 31, only one goal was scored—by Punch Broadbent—and the Senators made it stand up. Edmonton had come close, but they went home second best.

According to some sources, Simpson's nickname—Bullet Joe—

complimented his speed on the ice; others attributed the moniker to his war experiences. Either way, the name stuck. Bullet Joe played another two All-Star seasons in Edmonton before being dealt to the New York Americans of the NHL in 1925. Thirty-two years old at the time of the trade, Simpson would spend the rest of his playing career in the Big Apple.

He was never again an All-Star, but Simpson established himself as a reliable member of the Americans' blue line corps over the course of six hockey campaigns. The best of them was the 1928–29 season, when the Americans finished second in their division but lost in the first round of the playoffs to their cross-town rivals, the New York Rangers.

By the end of the 1930–31 campaign—another unsuccessful one for the Americans—Bullet Joe was thirty-seven. He had scored only two goals in forty-two games. He hung up his skates, but he wasn't finished with hockey. After taking a year off, he returned to the Americans in a new role: coach.

Sadly for the pride of Selkirk, the Americans were on the wrong end of a losing record in all three of his coaching years in New York. His team won just forty-two times in 144 scheduled games over the period. Simpson continued as a coach in minor pro hockey—in New Haven, Minneapolis, and Miami—before deciding to end his hockey career in 1939, just as another war erupted.

Bullet Joe is yet another member of the Hockey Hall of Fame draft of 1962—and he lived long enough to savour the honour. The former New Yorker must have liked what he had seen of south Florida in his time as coach of the Miami Clippers, because when he died aged eighty on Christmas Day, 1973, he was in Coral Gables, Florida.

There is another tribute that might have meant something to Bullet Joe. On the grounds of the Marine Museum of Manitoba at Selkirk is a small fleet of antique vessels linked by walkways for the benefit of visitors keen to learn about the region's nautical history. One of the ships is a small, flat-bottomed lake freighter that was restored and given a new name: *Joe Simpson*.

Moose Goheen

Mad for Minnesota

ALL-TIME GREATS

MOOSE GOHEEN

1960–61 Topps All-Time Greats

St. Paul Athletic Club/
White Bear Lakers/
U.S. Olympic Team/
St. Paul Saints (1914–32)

U.S. Army Signal Corps (1917–19)

Hockey Hall of Fame (1952)

★ ★ ★

Wouldn't a hockey player going by the nickname Moose necessarily have to be a Canadian? Perhaps not. Francis Xavier Goheen grew up a little more than four hundred miles south of the Forty-Ninth Parallel in chilly White Bear Lake, Minnesota.

Like his compatriot Hobey Baker, Goheen was a multitalented athlete, excelling at football and baseball as well as hockey. But where Baker seemed to have been born with extraordinary athletic ability, Goheen painstakingly developed his by a combination of hard work and determination.

Moose was an amateur for much of his hockey career, starting with his first team, St. Paul Athletic Club, in 1914. One of his teammates, Tony Conroy, laid claim to having blessed Goheen with the honorific Moose. Perhaps exaggerating a little, Conroy described his comrade as having a chest as big as a house and thighs as big as another teammate's waist. But it wasn't just Goheen's size that impressed Conroy—he rhapsodized about Moose's remarkable speed and competitiveness too.

In 1916, St. Paul AC won the American amateur championship, thereby earning the McNaughton Cup, the U.S. counterpart to Canada's Allan Cup.

In April 1917, the United States entered the Great War. Goheen did his bit for Uncle Sam by enlisting in the U.S. Army Signal Corps. Capitalizing on the skills he had acquired from working for a power company in Minnesota, he laid telephone wire over ground captured from the enemy in the battlefields of Belgium. He managed to carry out his soldierly duties without coming to serious harm and returned to the North Star State in 1919.

In 1920, hockey became an Olympic sport for the first time. Four members of St. Paul AC were included on the U.S. team, one of them barrel-chested Moose Goheen. The Games were played in Antwerp in August and September, as the separate Winter Games had not yet been established.

The Americans did very well for themselves. They capped 7–0 and 16–0 victories over Sweden and Czechoslovakia with a 29–0 demolition of Switzerland. But in order to claim the hockey championship, they also had to deal with the Canadians—and that wasn't quite so easy. In the semi-final, no doubt helped by four of their number being Canadian-born players who had mastered the game in their native land, the Americans did very well against Canada but came out on the short end of a 2–0 score. Though his team had to make do with a silver medal, no one could pin the blame on Moose Goheen: he was the team leader and scored seven goals in the Americans' four games.

1920 USA Olympic Hockey Team, **Moose Goheen**, seventh left

Two years after his fine Olympic performance, Goheen took his skills to the St. Paul Saints. Initially a club in the U.S. Amateur Hockey Association, the Saints were one of the teams in the short-lived Central Hockey League for one season and then, in 1926–27, became a charter member of a new minor pro league, the American Hockey Association. The AHA included three Minnesota clubs and one team each in Winnipeg, Chicago, and Detroit. At the grand old age of thirty-two, Moose Goheen was a hockey pro for the first time.

Over the course of eight seasons with the Saints, Goheen was a league All-Star six times. He was good enough to be offered professional contracts with at least two NHL organizations—the Boston Bruins and the Toronto Maple Leafs—but he was still appreciated by St. Paul hockey fans and had another reason for preferring to stay close to home. He was not just a hockey player but an entirely happy employee of the Northern States Power Company.

In 1924, Moose was invited to join the U.S. Olympic hockey team for a second time, but rather than travel to Chamonix for another chance at a gold medal, he decided his loyalty lay with his employer and he stayed home. Without the pride of White Bear Lake on the ice, the 1924 result mirrored that of 1920: the Americans lost narrowly to the Canadians and had to settle once again for the silver medal.

Goheen's best AHA season was 1927–28: that year he notched nineteen goals in thirty-nine games, third best in the league.

With the exception of a brief fling with the Buffalo Majors in 1930–31, Goheen played his entire career—amateur and professional—in the state of Minnesota. He took his final turn back in St. Paul, with the Saints, before hanging up his skates at age thirty-seven in 1932.

In 1950, a panel of hockey experts judged Goheen to be the best hockey player ever produced in the state of Minnesota. The legendary Lester Patrick, hockey innovator extraordinaire, went further, calling Moose the greatest U.S. player of all time.

These accolades were trumped by another honour in 1952. That year, Moose became only the second American—after Hobey Baker—elected to the Hockey Hall of Fame. Goheen would eventually be honoured with two more Hall-of-Fame inductions: the Minnesota Sports Hall of Fame in 1958 and the U.S. Hockey Hall of Fame in 1973.

Francis Xavier "Moose" Goheen lived long enough to savour all three appointments. Thriving in the air of Minnesota, he endured well into his eighty-sixth year before dying in 1979 in Maplewood. Maplewood? It's in Minnesota, of course.

The Many Hats of
Jolly Jack Adams

★ JACK ADAMS ★

Toronto Arenas/Vancouver Millionaires/
Toronto St. Patricks/
Ottawa Senators (1916–27)

Canadian Railway Troops Depot (1918)

Hockey Hall of Fame (1959)

★ ★ ★

J ohn James (Jack) Adams was just fourteen when he began making a name for himself as a hockey player on the north shore of Lake Superior in his home town, Fort William. His early hockey résumé included stints with his high school—Fort William Collegiate—as well as the local YMCA team.

At age twenty in 1915, he went to Michigan to play a season with the Calumet Miners of the Northern Michigan Senior Hockey League. The NMSHL seems to have been a precursor of the league featured in the hugely popular 1977 movie *Slap Shot*—a hockey circuit whose stock-in-trade was mayhem and violence. Young Adams survived his season at Calumet but returned to Canada with considerably more scar tissue than when he'd left.

Though not yet a soldier in the Canadian Expeditionary Force (CEF), Adams played for the Peterborough 247th Battalion team in 1916–17 and for the Sarnia Sailors of the Ontario Hockey Association (OHA) in '17–18. He then turned pro, playing eight games with the NHL Toronto Arenas in 1918. In his first year as a pro, he was a Stanley Cup winner. The Arenas were league champions in the first year of the NHL's existence, and then they capped that success with a Stanley Cup victory over the Vancouver Millionaires of the Pacific Coast Hockey Association (PCHA).

Having been disinclined to volunteer for service in the CEF, Adams was ultimately deprived of any choice in the matter. Conscripted under the *Military Service Act*, Adams completed his MSA attestation at London, Ontario, in March 1918. It was a rare hockey player who identified himself as such in addressing the question "What is your trade or calling?" Adams gave his occupation as *grain elevator weighman* and named his father as next-of-kin.

Adams embarked for England the following month and was assigned to a railway construction company, but there is little in his service record to indicate that he had an eventful time in England. His medical record refers to a hospital stay for the treatment of a neck abscess in the latter half of April, but there is no evidence that Corporal Adams needed medical intervention of the sort required by Punch Broadbent and Joe Simpson.

In further contrast to Broadbent and Simpson, Adams did not earn any awards for gallantry. But there is no indication of poor conduct either. In his Discharge Certificate, under the heading Character and Conduct, Adams was assessed as *Very Good* by his commanding officer.

The war turned out to be only a hiccup in Adams's hockey career. He was discharged from the army in November 1918, early enough that he was able to play most of the 1918–19 season with the Arenas.

Though his numbers in Toronto were not exceptional—three goals and three assists in seventeen games—Frank Patrick must have liked what he had seen of Adams in the 1917–18 Stanley Cup final, before he had been conscripted. The Vancouver owner acquired Adams, now twenty-four, for a significant sum.

Adams flourished in the PCHA. He was a league first-team All-Star in both 1921 and 1922. In the 1921–22 campaign, Jack led the PCHA in scoring with twenty-six goals in twenty-four games.

Vancouver played for the Stanley Cup in 1921, but Adams's Millionaires lost to Punch Broadbent's Ottawa Senators. A year later, Vancouver reached the Cup final again. Adams led the scoring parade with twenty-six goals in twenty-four games—ten better than Frank Foyston—but the Millionaires were losers again, this time to the Toronto St. Patricks.

For players, hockey in the 1920s was not as nearly lucrative as it would become many decades later, but they did have much more freedom to go wherever they wished and skate with whomever they wanted. The St. Patricks must have liked what they'd seen of Adams in the 1922 final and he must have been given an offer he couldn't refuse, because he took bag and baggage to Toronto and, by mid-December, he was playing alongside the men who had been his adversaries just months before.

Adams played four years in Toronto. He did well—twenty-one goals in each of the 1924–25 and '25–26 seasons—but his star did not shine quite as brightly as it had done in Vancouver's Denman Street Arena. He was not named an All-Star in any of his Toronto years.

In 1926, he was dealt by Toronto to the Ottawa Senators. The 1926–27 season was a good one to be in Ottawa. The Senators finished the regular schedule with the league's best record and went on to win the Stanley Cup in a final series against the Boston Bruins. It was Adams's second and the Senators' eleventh Cup victory. But Adams, now in his thirty-second year, had slipped more than a little: in forty games with the Senators he managed only five goals. He called it quits as a player.

Adams had acquired a nickname that was perhaps not as evocative as Punch or Bullet Joe but that reflected well on his effusive nature—Jolly Jack. His playing career had been outstanding enough that he could take considerable pride in it, but it was in the years after his playing days that Adams made his biggest mark in hockey.

In 1927, he was appointed coach of the Detroit Cougars, a club reconstituted from the Victoria Cougars when the western league was disbanded in 1926. Adams succeeded Art Duncan—a decorated war hero and Canadian ace fighter pilot—as Detroit coach. Detroit, winners of only eleven of forty-four games under Duncan in 1926–27, improved to nineteen victories during Adams's first year behind the bench. Mediocre in the next four seasons, the Red Wings—the Cougars had been renamed the Falcons in 1930, and subsequently renamed again in 1932—took a leap forward in '32–33. Detroit finished second in the American Division before losing to Chicago in the Stanley Cup semi-final.

Finally, in 1935–36—Adams's ninth year as coach—the Red Wings were Stanley Cup champions, defeating the Toronto Maple Leafs 3–1 in a best-of-five final. Adams would do it again a year later, this time over the New York Rangers, 3–2.

Adams would taste one more Cup victory as coach. The Red Wings won again in 1943, with a four-game sweep of the Boston Bruins. It was Adams's fifth Cup victory—two as a player, three as a coach.

The 1946–47 season, Adams's twentieth as the Red Wings coach, was also his last. He moved upstairs to the general manager's office just as a young fellow from Saskatchewan named Gordie Howe was starting what would be a long, outstanding career as a Detroit Red Wing.

As Red Wings GM, Jolly Jack enjoyed even greater success. The Red Wings were Stanley Cup winners in 1950, 1952, 1954, and 1955—all with Jack Adams calling the shots from the Detroit front office.

While successful as a general manager, Adams was not always jolly. He could be ruthless too, as exemplified by a new role that he added to his résumé: union buster. In 1957, he offloaded Ted Lindsay, a key player in the Red Wings' 1950s success, because of Lindsay's efforts to organize NHL players into a union. Adams alienated other key players and eventually wore out his welcome in the Motor City. He was fired in 1963 after a combined thirty-six years as Detroit coach and general manager—the longest such stretch in NHL history.

By 1955 he had won two Stanley Cups as a player, three as a coach, and four as a GM. He is the only man to have had his name inscribed on the Cup in all three capacities. He could just as easily have been enshrined in the Builders Division of the Hockey Hall of Fame, but it was as a player that Adams was inducted in 1959. In 1974, the NHL established a trophy to honour the league's coach of the year—the Jack Adams Memorial Trophy.

Following his forced retirement in 1963, Jolly Jack Adams had five years to contemplate more than a half century in hockey—the good, the bad, and the not-so-jolly. He died in his seventy-third year in Detroit in 1968.

Conn Smythe

Eight-Time Stanley Cup Winner

★ CONN SMYTHE ★

Canadian Field Artillery (1915–19)

Toronto Maple Leafs Coach, Manager, and Owner (1927–62)

Hockey Hall of Fame (1958)

★ ★ ★

Constantine (Conn) Falkland Cary Smythe, born February 1, 1895, fashioned himself into an able athlete in several sports—football, basketball, and hockey—while attending Jarvis Collegiate Institute in 1912. By 1914, he was an engineering student at the University of Toronto.

Smythe managed to find time away from his scholarly endeavours not only to play hockey but also to manage the U of T varsity hockey team. In 1915, just days after his team won the OHA junior title, Smythe and everyone else on the Varsity squad volunteered for overseas service in the Canadian Expeditionary Force. He was nineteen when he enlisted in a unit of the Canadian Field Artillery.

Captain Conn Smythe

By the autumn of 1916, Smythe's 40th Battery was in the thick of the fighting in the Battle of the Somme. Resisting a German counterattack, he dispatched three enemy soldiers and helped rescue several wounded compatriots. For his actions in this affair, Captain Smythe was awarded the Military Cross (MC), the counterpart for commissioned officers of the Military Medal awarded to lower ranks.

Commending his "conspicuous gallantry," Smythe's MC citation reports him as having led his men "with great dash, thereby dispersing an enemy party at a critical time." He received his MC on April 25, 1917, two weeks after the Canadian victory at Vimy Ridge.

Despite his soldierly courage and ability having been recognized in this way, by the spring of 1917, Smythe had decided that there must be something better than the life of a front-line artilleryman. He therefore sought and got a reassignment—to the Royal Flying Corps (RFC).

In late May 1917, he was attached to the RFC as an "observer on probation." On June 5, he was appointed flying officer. One of the officers under whom Smythe learned to fly was the Canadian flier ace William Barker, the most decorated Canadian serviceman of the Great War and someone who would eventually become the first president of an NHL hockey club, the Toronto Maple Leafs, partly owned by Smythe.

In mid-autumn 1917, Smythe's fortunes took a turn for the worse. On October 14, as the Canada Corps was preparing to take on the German divisions dug in along Passchendaele Ridge, Smythe went missing in action.

He had been flying as an air observer, directing artillery crews on where to aim their fire, when his machine was downed by the enemy. He survived the crash landing but was captured and sent to a German prisoner of war camp at Schweidnitz in Upper Silesia, where he spent the rest of the war. He did not endure captivity passively: on at least two occasions he attempted an escape. Neither attempt succeeded, but when the war was over Smythe was mentioned in reports and commended "for valuable services whilst in captivity."

Smythe was released from his prisoner of war camp and repatriated to England in late December 1918. Finally, in March 1919, he was back in Canada.

Upon returning home, Smythe initially sought to establish himself in the sand and gravel business. In his spare time, he renewed his connection with the University of Toronto hockey team. The U of T skaters occasionally travelled to New England to play U.S. college sides. Smythe made connections in Boston, one of which culminated in his being offered the job of building a contending roster for a new NHL team, the New York Rangers.

Smythe had barely warmed his front office chair before he was sent packing by the Rangers owner, Tex Rickard. Smythe blamed his dismissal on Rickard's displeasure with his manager's decision not to go along with the boss's wish to sign Babe Dye. But was that the real reason Smythe was sacked? When the Western Hockey League (*Canada* was dropped from the league name for the 1925–26 season) collapsed at the end of that season, a hockey luminary was suddenly available to run a club: Lester Patrick. Whatever the real reason behind Smythe's being let go, it was Patrick who took on the management of the Rangers. In 1928, the Rangers won the Stanley Cup—largely on the backs of players signed by Smythe during his short New York tenure.

A mover and shaker of the first rank, Smythe played a key role in organizing a syndicate that raised the capital necessary to buy the Toronto St. Patricks in 1927. In short order he arranged to wear four hats for the club: part-owner, league governor, general manager, and coach. One of his early initiatives was to change the team name—from the St. Patricks to the Maple Leafs.

Toronto Maple Leafs 1927–28 logo

According to the Maple Leafs website, the name change came about because Smythe wanted to honour a Canadian Expeditionary Force unit named the Maple Leaf Regiment. There was no such regiment. But it is well established that Smythe was a patriot, proud of the Canada Corps and his role in it during the war. The maple leaf *was* a key emblem of the entire Canada Corps; it was incorporated in the badges worn by soldiers in a great many Canadian battalions.

Finally, it is a maple leaf that adorns the grave marker of every soldier, known and unknown, buried in the war cemeteries of Belgium and France. It seems highly likely that by choosing the maple leaf as his hockey team's emblem, Smythe meant to honour not a single unit but the entire Canada Corps.

Smythe's Military Cross had demonstrated that he was a willing warrior, and he certainly proved to be a combative coach and manager in the NHL. His famed operating principle in choosing men to play for the Leafs—"If you can't beat 'em in the alley, you can't beat 'em on the ice"—serves just as well in summing up his whole approach to building a winning hockey team. He exhibited no inclination to be a "nice guy" and likely agreed entirely with the dictum of his contemporary, the long-time baseball manager Leo Durocher: "Nice guys finish last."

Smythe coached his club for three seasons, from 1927 to 1931, and then turned the coaching reins over to Art Duncan, a twice-decorated Canadian ace flier. Perhaps Duncan was too nice: Smythe relieved him after a single season, replacing him with Dick Irvin. Meanwhile, Smythe was a whirlwind: despite being kept busy managing the hockey team, he was instrumental in building a new Toronto arena—Maple Leaf Gardens—in 1931.

Irvin won a Stanley Cup on his first try in 1931–32 and got the Leafs to the Cup finals—albeit without winning—six times between 1933 and 1940. Hap Day took over in 1941 and coached Toronto to five Stanley Cups in the 1940s.

When Canada went to war again, in 1939, Conn Smythe stepped forward once more. Serving as an officer in Canada in the early years of the Second World War, he shipped out first to England in 1942 and then to France in 1944. He was seriously wounded in France when a German bomb destroyed a nearby ammunition depot. He suffered wounds that afflicted him for the rest of his life.

By the mid-1950s, the Leafs' fortunes had declined. Smythe handed over management to others, including his son Stafford. It was an often tempestuous arrangement, as Conn Smythe was either unable or unwilling to let others run the team. He remained combative and obstreperous—and increasingly reactionary—as he approached old age. Like Jack Adams, he was a union buster, fiercely resistant to players' efforts to unionize for better wages and conditions.

But there is no disputing that, between 1932 and 1962, Smythe's name was inscribed on the Stanley Cup eight times. In 1964, a new trophy was established to honour the player judged to have been the most valuable player in the Stanley Cup playoffs: the Conn Smythe Trophy. He was inducted in the Hockey Hall of Fame the same year that so many other soldier-players were admitted to the pantheon: 1958. And he had plenty of time to enjoy the honour. Smythe died in Toronto well into his eighty-sixth year—a war hero, coach, manager, and part-owner of one of the storied franchises of the NHL.

Duke Keats

Even Capone Was a Fan

**Toronto Blueshirts/Edmonton Eskimos/
Boston Bruins/Detroit Red Wings/
Chicago Blackhawks** (1915–29)

**228th Infantry Battalion/6th Battalion,
Canadian Railway Troops** (1916–19)

Hockey Hall of Fame (1958)

★ ★ ★

★ DUKE KEATS ★

Were there a gallery in Toronto's Hockey Hall of Fame devoted to players distinguished by individualism, force of personality, and the sheer, riotous colour of their character, it is hard to conceive of a man who would have a higher place in its pantheon than Gordon Blanchard "Duke" Keats.

A Montrealer by birth, young Gordon Keats earned his early hockey chops in the rough-and-tumble mining country of northern Ontario. Nowadays a town of not much more than a thousand residents, Cobalt, Ontario, emerged from the boreal forest on the strength of its rich silver and cobalt deposits. It was there that Keats inaugurated his amateur hockey career at age seventeen with the Cobalt McKinley Mines club in 1912–13. A year later he switched allegiance to another team of hockey-playing miners—the Cobalt O'Brien Mines club—then moved more than ninety miles south to further develop his game with the North Bay Trappers of the Northern Ontario Hockey Association (NOHA).

In 1914–15, Keats headed back north for a gig with the Haileybury Hawks of the Thunder Bay Senior Hockey League (TBSHL). Having served a three-year apprenticeship in amateur hockey, he decided to seek his fortune in pro hockey. For the '15–16 season, he reached for the top, signing a contract to play for the 1914 Stanley Cup champions, the Toronto Blueshirts of the NHA. He had just turned twenty.

Toronto did not repeat its 1914 success: the Blueshirts finished dead last in the five-team National Hockey Association (NHA), but no one could pin the blame on Keats. He played splendidly for Toronto, leading the team in scoring with twenty-two goals and twenty-nine points in

228th Battalion Northern Fusiliers, **Duke Keats**, second left, standing; **Percy LeSueur**, second right, standing

the twenty-four–game regular schedule. He also led the team in penalty minutes with 112, close to five minutes a game. Included among Keats's 1915–16 teammates were Percy LeSueur and Frank Foyston.

Three months after the close of the 1915–16 season, Keats volunteered for overseas service with the Canadian Expeditionary Force. By June 1916 he had returned to North Bay, and it was there that he enlisted in the 228th Battalion. He is unique among the thirty soldier-players who would one day be inducted in the Hall of Fame. To the question "What is your trade or calling?" Keats answered *professional hockey player.*

As noted elsewhere, bright lights in the army's higher command had what seemed a compelling idea: Why not mobilize a team of talented hockey players, get them into hockey's premier pro league, have them succeed, and thereby induce young impressionable men into doing their bit for King and Country? And that is how the 228th Northern Fusiliers came to join the NHA for the 1916–17 season. They played well and were popular with hockey fans. As for the number of young fellows persuaded to become soldiers, that is not known.

A portrait of the Fusiliers has survived. In it nine players, all in military uniforms rather than hockey sweaters, are gathered around their commanding officer. In years to come, three of the players—LeSueur, George McNamara, and Keats—would be elected to the Hockey Hall of Fame. But that was a matter for the future. In the present, Keats would become the rope in a tug-of-war between the military and the managers of the Toronto Blueshirts.

As part of the deal admitting the Northern Fusiliers to the NHA, the military bosses agreed to let two of their men—Keats and LeSueur—fulfill their existing obligations to Toronto and play for the Blueshirts rather than the Fusiliers in 1916–17.

As it turned out, LeSueur, thirty-five at the time, ending up playing for no one. He retired from the game and turned his attention to his new military duties—instructing soldiers in the efficient use of the bayonet. Keats *did* play—for the Blueshirts—but as often as they could arrange it, senior officers saw to it that he was burdened with duties whenever he was scheduled to play for the Blueshirts. As a result, he played in only thirteen of Toronto's twenty-four scheduled games, but he played superbly, scoring fifteen goals in those thirteen games. The 228th faced the Blueshirts three times during the season—and won twice.

Private Gordon Keats

The Northern Fusiliers played their last game February 7, 1917. Deciding they needed soldiers more than hockey players, the military bosses folded the team on or around February 10, 1917. Nine days later, the 228th embarked for England and the war. Originally conceived as an infantry battalion, the 228th was reconstituted as the 6th Battalion, Canadian Railway Troops, and its men were employed in railway construction and repair for the duration of the war.

The most eye-catching item in Keats's war service record is an entry for January 10, 1918. On that day he was sentenced to fourteen days' Field Punishment No. 1, evidently for drunkenness. Soldiers loathed Field Punishment No. 1, and no wonder. It included being tied to a wheel or other fixed object for two hours a day.

Duke Keats/Edmonton Eskimos

Nothing else in Keats's war record is so eventful. In March 1919 he was aboard HMT *Celtic*, en route back to Canada.

Keats moved west for the 1919–20 season and threw in his lot with the Edmonton Eskimos of the top-flight amateur Big-4 League. It was the beginning of a productive collaboration. Over the course of seven years in the Alberta capital, two in the Big-4, five in a new pro circuit named the Western Canada Hockey League (WCHL), he was an All-Star five times.

Duke Keats/Chicago Blackhawks

Due to his strength and durability, Keats was nicknamed Iron Duke, or simply Duke, after British warships of the late nineteenth and early twentieth centuries—three of them—that bore the name. In 1921–22, he was a wunderkind. He tallied thirty-one goals and twenty-four assists in twenty-five games— a fifty-five–point total that left the second-best scorer twenty-two points in arrears. In four of those seasons between 1919 and 1926, one of Keats's teammates was Bullet Joe Simpson.

In 1926, now aged thirty-one, Keats was dealt to the NHL Boston Bruins for cash. He played only briefly for the Bruins before being traded to Detroit for Frank Fredrickson. Though not as eye-catching as the numbers he had put together in Edmonton, Keats was effective in Detroit, scoring twelve times in twenty-five games with the Cougars.

Just five games into the 1927–28 season, with Jolly Jack Adams behind the Detroit bench, Keats took exception to a fan's throwing a drink on him. He went into the stands and, in the process of delivering retribution unto the fan, came close to injuring an innocent bystander—Irene Castle, a famous actress of her time. Unsurprisingly, this made Keats *persona non grata* in Detroit. He was subsequently dealt to the Chicago Blackhawks, whose owner, Major Frederic McLaughlin, just happened to be the spouse of Irene Castle. Clearly, the major harboured no grudge.

The Iron Duke did well for himself in Chicago, with fourteen goals and twenty-two points in his thirty-two games in the Windy City. He also made new fans.

One night, annoyed at being followed on the street by two men in dark suits, Keats turned on them and demanded to know what they were up to. No mischief, the men explained, "Mr. Capone just wants to make sure you get home safely, Duke." Even America's most famous gangster loved Keats.

Chicago turned out to be Keats's last stop as a major league player. The following season, 1928–29, he was sold for cash to a minor pro team. He hung on for a few seasons of minor pro hockey before quitting for good at age thirty-nine in 1934.

Gordon Keats was inducted in the Hockey Hall of Fame in 1958, together with Frank Foyston, Herb Gardiner, Dick Irvin, George McNamara, and Frank Fredrickson. He lived for another fourteen years before dying in January 1972, in his seventy-seventh year.

His final resting place is a hilltop in the upper reaches of Royal Oak Burial Ground in Victoria, British Columbia. For the passerby who knows nothing of Gordon Keats, there is a hint as to who he was: the granite grave marker features a pair of crossed hockey sticks. The gravesite commands a fine view over the valley below—a vantage point fit for a king, or at least a duke. Just down the hill there is the grave of another Hockey Hall-of-Famer, the legendary Lester Patrick, who once called Gordon Keats "the brainiest pivot that ever strapped on a skate."

The Luck of Frank Fredrickson,
Pride of Iceland

★ F. FREDRICKSON ★

Winnipeg Falcons/
Victoria Cougars/
Detroit Cougars/
Boston Bruins (1913–31)

223rd Battalion/Royal Flying Corps/
Royal Air Force (1916–19)

Hockey Hall of Fame (1958)

★ ★ ★

His blue eyes and fair complexion notwithstanding, Sigurdur Frank Fredrickson experienced discrimination in his early years in Winnipeg. Born in Canada, Fredrickson was the son of parents who had immigrated to Manitoba from Iceland toward the end of the nineteenth century. He spoke only Icelandic before he went to school.

They ate different food, went to a different church, and spoke accented English, but Fredrickson and his friends were perfectly Canadian in their enthusiasm for the game of hockey. Shunned by lads of other ethnic origins, the Icelanders organized themselves into hockey teams of their own. Soon enough they were beating everyone in sight.

By age eighteen, in 1913, Fredrickson was the leading light of the Winnipeg Falcons, virtually all them ethnic Icelanders. That year, their first in the Independent Hockey League (IHL), the Falcons finished last. It took only a year for them to reverse their fortunes: in 1914–15 they won the league championship.

In February 1916, Fredrickson—known to all by now as Frank, rather than Sigurdur—volunteered for the Canadian Expeditionary Force. He enlisted in the 196th Battalion but soon moved to the 223rd Battalion (Canadian Scandinavians). Enrolled in the University of Manitoba at the time, he listed his "trade or calling" as *student*.

The 223rd iced a team for the 1916-17 MSHL season. Playing with the Falcons, Fredrickson had led the MSHL in scoring the previous year; he did it again in 1916–17, with seventeen goals in just eight games.

The 223rd embarked from Halifax in early May 1917, arriving in Liverpool May 15. It didn't take long before Frederickson decided that the life of a foot soldier in an infantry battalion might not be the best option on offer in King George's combined forces. He decided to

Frank Fredrickson in Egypt

become an airman and, together with two fellow Falcons, managed to get a transfer to the Royal Flying Corps (RFC).

Aboard the troopship *Aragon*, the Icelanders departed Taranto, Italy, for Alexandria, Egypt, to do their air training. Shortly after their safe passage, the *Aragon* was torpedoed by a German U-boat, which resulted in the loss of more than six hundred lives.

While learning to fly at the British airbase in Aboukir, the Winnipeggers managed to squeeze more than a little fun into their days. Fredrickson took a camera wherever he went; photographs taken during his time in Aboukir show him at the Sphinx, riding a camel, and wearing his airman uniform but with an Egyptian fez on his head. There is a standard feature in every image—Fredrickson's beaming smile.

In May, his flight training successfully completed, Fredrickson departed Alexandria for the return voyage across the Mediterranean. He had avoided disaster on his outward journey but he was unluckier this time: on May 28, the transport ship he was travelling on, the *Leasowe Castle*, was struck by a German torpedo. Ninety-two men were lost.

Fredrickson was a highly accomplished violinist. As men fled the sinking *Leasowe Castle*, he put his cherished violin in the hands of a lifeboat captain. There was no room for Fredrickson, but once in the water he managed to scramble into a different lifeboat. The violin was saved—and so was Fredrickson.

Once in Britain, he was posted to a Royal Air Force airbase in Gullane, Scotland. The average life expectancy of a fighter pilot operating over the Western Front was less than twenty hours of flying time, but Fredrickson struck lucky again. Because he was a talented flier and able communicator, his commanders decided the best use the RAF could make of him was as a flying instructor and test pilot.

He flew an array of machines: the Sopwith Camel and Pup, Bristol Fighter, Nieuports, and the superb new Royal Aircraft Factory scout, the SE5A.

As he had done at Aboukir, Fredrickson made a point of balancing duty with fun. Charmed by a young Edinburgh woman, Fredrickson

Lieutenant Frank Fredrickson, Royal Air Force

decided to do some "sensational flying" over a tea party she had arranged. On returning to Gullane, the engine of his SE5A failed. He crash-landed, sustaining multiple and widespread cuts, contusions, and bruises. But he survived again.

Gullane was close enough to Edinburgh that Fredrickson was able to take frequent advantage of the city's amenities, and he attended many theatrical events and concerts. He was a capable photographer and took impressive images of Edinburgh landmarks and kept a diary record-ing detailed impressions of the city and the urban attractions he liked best. While flying out of Gullane, he experienced the occasional hair-raising landing but suffered nothing worse than bruises and lacerations. November 11 brought the end of the war: Fredrickson had come through.

He returned to Canada in time to resume playing for the Winnipeg Falcons in 1919–20. He hadn't lost a step, once again leading the league in scoring with twenty-three goals in just ten games. After establishing themselves as the best team in Manitoba, the Falcons took on the University of Toronto for the Canadian amateur championship—and the Allan Cup. They won easily, outscoring U of T 11–5 in a two-game series.

On the strength of that victory, the Falcons earned the right to represent Canada in the first Olympic Games that included hockey. Fredrickson and the Falcons travelled to Antwerp, Belgium, for the 1920 Games. In the quarter-final against Czechoslovakia, the Canadians won easily, 15–0. The semi-final was tougher, as they were facing Moose Goheen and his fellow Americans, but the Canadians won, 2–0. The gold medal game against Sweden was a cakewalk: a 12–1 victory.

Iceland could take as much pride in the gold medal as Canada did: the Canadians were almost entirely sons of Icelandic immigrants, men named Johannesson, Halderson, Fridfinnson—and Fredrickson. The boys with odd-sounding names had turned themselves into world champions.

As this great adventure was drawing to a close, Fredrickson was offered another. He learned that an Icelandic company was looking for an ethnic Icelander to introduce people to flying. Fredrickson seized the opportunity to travel to the land of his forbears and take Icelanders into the air in a 504K Avro. While in Iceland, he crash-landed—and survived—again.

1920 Canadian Olympic Hockey Team, **Frank Fredrickson**, fifth left

One more great adventure lay in store. Mulling his options at age twenty-six, Fredrickson was contemplating a career in the Royal Canadian Air Force (RCAF). Then Lester Patrick made him an offer he couldn't refuse: $2,500 to play a twenty-four–game season with his Victoria club in the PCHA. Fredrickson agreed.

What followed was a storied six-year career in British Columbia's capital. The pride of Icelandic Winnipeg led his club in scoring all six years and was a league All-Star in all but one of those years. In 1922–23, he scored thirty-nine goals and added sixteen assists to win the league scoring title by eighteen points over the second-best scorer. In 1925, he led the Victoria Cougars to a Stanley Cup victory over the Montreal Canadiens. It was the last time a club not part of the NHL would have its name inscribed on the Cup.

Fredrickson had one more kick at the Cup the following year, 1925–26, but this time the Cougars lost to the Montreal Maroons. It was a finale for the league too: the Western Hockey League folded after the Stanley Cup series.

1925 Victoria Cougars

In 1926–27, Fredrickson and several of his Victoria teammates found themselves reconstituted as the Detroit Cougars of the NHL. Fredrickson reached another pinnacle: earning $6,000 for the '26–27 season, he was the highest-paid player in pro hockey. He played only sixteen games in Detroit before he was parcelled up and shipped to the Boston Bruins for Gordon Keats.

In his thirties by this time, Fredrickson would not shine in the NHL quite as brightly as he had done in Victoria. He played three years in Boston and liked his situation there, but in 1928, he was dealt to the Pittsburgh Pirates. He played two seasons there before returning to Detroit for one final go-round in 1930–31. By age thirty-five he was done.

In 1929–30, while still a player, Fredrickson had taken over as Pittsburgh coach. The new role was not rewarding: the Pirates won only five times in a forty-four–game schedule and finished twenty-one points behind next-worst Detroit. The following year, the franchise was moved to Philadelphia and Fredrickson was replaced as coach by none other than Cooper Smeaton.

In 1933, Fredrickson accepted a job as coach of Hobey Baker's alma mater, Princeton University. There was another Princeton rookie that year, a physicist-mathematician who had decided that Adolf Hitler's Germany was no longer a tolerable place to call home. The learned man had something in common with Fredrickson: he too was an accomplished violinist. They struck up a friendship and often walked to campus together. The other violinist? Albert Einstein.

When the Second World War erupted in 1939, Fredrickson stepped forward again. He joined the RCAF, commanded an air force flying school, and coached an air force hockey team, the Sea Island Flyers, from 1940 until 1945. After the war he took over as coach of the University of British Columbia and was highly regarded by the Thunderbirds who played for him.

Another member of the Hockey Hall of Fame class of 1958, Frank Fredrickson lived long and well. He died two weeks short of his eighty-fourth birthday, in Vancouver, in 1979.

Phat Wilson

Amateur Purist

141st Battalion HC/
Port Arthur War Vets HC/
Port Arthur Bearcats (1915–32)

Hockey Hall of Fame (1962)

★ ★ ★

Gordon Allan "Phat" Wilson was a celebrated baseball player in and around his home town of Port Arthur, Ontario, in the years before the Great War. He came to hockey late, learning to skate only in 1914, by which time he was already eighteen years old.

Like Hobey Baker, he was clearly a quick learner and made himself as proficient in hockey as he was in baseball. In the 1915–16 season, he was accomplished enough to play in the Thunder Bay Senior Hockey League (TBSHL) with the Port Arthur Shuniahs, a team named for a community that is now part of the city of Thunder Bay.

A year later, in 1916–17, Wilson played a single game with the hockey team of the 141st (Rainy River) Battalion of the Canadian Expeditionary Force. And that gives rise to a mystery. Had Wilson volunteered in the CEF? Had he enlisted in the 141st? Perhaps not: his name does not appear in the nominal roll of men who went off to war with the 141st. No less an authority than Veterans Affairs Canada includes Wilson in a list of Hockey Hall-of-Fame players who were also soldiers of the Great War. But the same list indicates that no military official records are to be found for Wilson in the Library and Archives Canada database of soldiers who volunteered, were conscripted, or served in the Great War. Search that database for Gordon Allan Wilson, born December 29, 1895, in Port Arthur, Ontario, or any variant that comes to mind—Alan Wilson, Gordon Allan, Wilson Gordon, take your pick—and an inquiry will come up empty.

There is a telling gap in the record of Wilson's hockey career: he appears to have *not* played in the 1917–18 season, when tens of thousands of young Canadian men were in Europe fighting in the war. It is easy to infer that he played no hockey that year because he was doing his soldierly duty for King and Country. But we do not know for sure.

The record of Wilson's hockey career also includes an intriguing entry for the 1920–21 season. A defenceman throughout his career, he scored eleven goals in fifteen games for a team in the Thunder Bay Senior Hockey League—the Port Arthur War Vets—an affiliation that could tempt even a cautious observer to imagine that Wilson might have been a war veteran.

And what of Wilson's nickname? How did he come to be known as Phat? What kind of a name is that? What does Phat mean? The Oxford English Dictionary tells us that "phat" means *excellent*, a fair descriptor of Wilson's hockey talents, but it also notes that the word dates back only to the 1970s—too late to explain its being bestowed on Wilson a half-century earlier.

We do know a good deal about Wilson the hockey player, though. It is clear that over the course of the thirteen years immediately follow-ing the 1918 Armistice he was not disadvantaged by having learned to skate only in his late teens. He became a star player in Thunder Bay amateur hockey circles.

For the 1921–22 season, Wilson travelled almost five hundred miles east to play for the Iroquois Falls Flyers of the NOHA. That was the only time in his hockey career that he played for a team not based in Port Arthur.

He may not have been a professional, but Phat made the big time: he was featured in a hockey card, No. 16 in the 1923 Famous Hockey Players series, produced by the Paulin candy company of Winnipeg.

Phat Wilson
1923 Paulin's V128-1 series

Though not as highly esteemed today, the Allan Cup was every bit as prized as the Stanley Cup in its heyday in the years prior to and following the Great War. Established in 1909, the Allan Cup took over the role originally assigned to the Stanley Cup—the silverware awarded to the best amateur hockey club in Canada.

In 1925, Wilson led the Port Arthur Hockey Club—better known as the Bearcats—to an Allan Cup victory over the University of Toronto. The Bearcats outscored their Toronto opponents 7–2 in a two-game series. A year later they repeated their victory, but this time the U of T skaters made it closer: one game was tied and Port Arthur narrowly won two to take the best-of-three series two games to one.

In 1927, the Toronto Varsity Grads savoured sweet payback. Again the games were close, again one game was tied, but the Grads won two of the other games to take possession of the Allan Cup.

The year 1928 was an interregnum, as neither the Bearcats nor the Toronto Grads reached the Allan Cup final, but in 1929, Wilson and his club were back in play for the Allan Cup. This time the Bearcats' eastern opponents were Montreal St.-François-Xavier. The Bearcats won yet again.

There would be one more opportunity to compete for the Allan Cup. In 1930, Port Arthur and Montreal met again, this time at the

Mutual Street Arena in Toronto. Montreal manhandled Port Arthur 6–0 in the first game. The Bearcats narrowed the gap in Game 2, losing 2–1, but it was the Montrealers who rejoiced in victory.

Over six years, Wilson had led the Bearcats to the Allan Cup final five times, with three Cup victories.

Wilson's hockey talents were abundant and conspicuous. Despite playing on defence, behind the blue line, he led the Thunder Bay league in assists three times. He had several offers to turn professional but rejected them all. He remained a purist his whole career—playing for the joy of the game rather than for cash.

He finally hung up his skates in 1932 at the advanced age of thirty-six. He remained in hockey as a coach, calling the shots behind the bench for the Bearcats and their subsequent incarnation as the Port Arthur Ports. In his home town, Wilson also took on the role of hockey administrator for a string of senior amateur clubs. He encouraged girls to play too and organized a hockey league for them, which made him a significant ground-breaker.

Lauded as a brilliant rushing defenceman blessed with remarkable athletic ability, Phat Wilson was inducted in the Hockey Hall of Fame in 1962, together with seven other players featured in this book. He had eight years to enjoy the honour. He died in Thunder Bay—where else?—in 1970, in his seventy-fifth year.

— 4 —

THIRD
PERIOD

Reg Noble

Seventeen Seasons on a Bad Foot

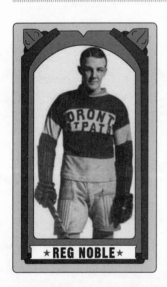

★ REG NOBLE ★

Toronto Blueshirts/Toronto Arenas/
Toronto St. Patricks/Montreal Maroons/
Detroit Cougars (1916–33)

180th Battalion,
Canadian Expeditionary Force (1916)

Hockey Hall of Fame (1962)

★ ★ ★

E dward Reginald (Reg) Noble launched his Hall-of-Fame hockey career in Simcoe County, Ontario, at the southern end of Georgian Bay. He started out at age sixteen in 1912 with the hometown Collingwood ACC club. After two seasons at Collingwood, he migrated more than ninety miles south to Toronto, where he played for St. Michael's College and the Riversides of the Ontario Hockey Association (OHA).

In early February 1916, Noble enlisted in the 180th (Sportsmen) Battalion, Canadian Expeditionary Force (CEF). He gave his "trade or calling" as *student*.

Noble's time in the 180th was short. He did not cross the Atlantic to do battle in the front lines of the Western Front. When the Sportsmen Battalion sailed for Europe on November 13, Noble was not aboard the troopship. Two months earlier he had been discharged from the CEF in surprising circumstances. Noble would go on to have a seventeen-year career in professional hockey, during which time he was regarded as a player with an iron constitution, but in September 1916 at Camp Borden, Ontario, military doctors determined that he was "medically unfit" for service overseas.

The reason for this assessment was a tendon in Noble's right foot that had previously been cut by a skate. One consequence of the old injury was that he had difficulty marching without frequent rests. The doctors tried, "but could do nothing for the condition." A foot soldier who couldn't march was problematic. He was relieved of his obligations to his country and to King George. His sportsmen comrades went off to war; Noble stayed home.

His damaged right foot may have disqualified Noble from long infantry marches, but it clearly presented no obstacle to his playing fourteen games for the Toronto Blueshirts in the 1916–17 National Hockey Association (NHA) season. The Blueshirts' scoring leader that season was the inestimable Duke Keats. Younger than Keats by more than a year, Noble was still a teenager—but a talented enough teenager to be Toronto's third-best scorer with seven goals in fourteen games.

The 1916–17 season was the NHA's last. A new circuit, the National Hockey League (NHL), was organized principally to outflank Eddie Livingstone, the Toronto owner, a man viewed as intolerably troublesome and vexatious by his fellow NHA owners. The Blueshirts were broken up and Noble was assigned to the Montreal Canadiens during the inaugural NHL season. A year later, he was back in Toronto with a new club, the Arenas.

In 1917–18, now aged twenty-one, Noble had a banner year in Toronto: he scored thirty goals in twenty games with the Arenas, good enough for third place among all NHL scorers. Toronto defeated

Reg Noble. 1924 William Patterson V145 series

Montreal for the NHL championship and then took on the Vancouver Millionaires for the Stanley Cup at Toronto's Mutual Street Arena. The Millionaires outscored Toronto 21–19 in the best-of-five series, but the Arenas won more games—and that was what mattered.

Noble's numbers were not nearly so impressive in 1918–19, and the defending Stanley Cup champions slipped to last place, winners of only five of eighteen regular-schedule games.

In 1919, new owners took over the Toronto franchise and bestowed a new name on the team—the St. Patricks. The team improved, winning half of their twenty-four scheduled games. Noble rebounded too, scoring twenty-four goals, fourth best in the NHL.

He continued to play at a high level for the St. Patricks for another five seasons. In 1921–22, he helped Toronto to another Stanley Cup victory. The losers were once again the Vancouver Millionaires, led by Jack Adams. Vancouver had played in the three of the four most recent Cup finals and lost them all.

By 1924 Noble had established himself as a bona fide NHL star: his image appeared on two hockey cards that year in the Champ's Cigarette and William Patterson series.

That same season, 1924, Noble was sold to the Montreal Maroons. In his early years he had played principally on the forward line in the centre position, but now he played more frequently behind the blue line as a defenceman.

In 1926, he completed a hat trick of sorts by winning his third Stanley Cup—a victory shared with teammate Punch Broadbent. The losing side was once again a west coast team, the Victoria Cougars, whose best player was Frank Fredrickson.

Noble continued to rely on the foot that was judged too damaged for the Canadian infantry but allowed him to star as an upper-echelon NHL skater.

Shortly after the 1926 Stanley Cup final, the Western Hockey League collapsed. The Victoria club Noble and Broadbent had defeated in April was reconstituted as the Detroit Cougars for the 1926–27 NHL season. Frank Fredrickson, who had been an opponent in April, was now Noble's teammate.

Though Fredrickson was soon dealt to Boston for Duke Keats, Noble played six seasons in Detroit, a period in which the franchise went through two name changes: from the Cougars to the Falcons, in 1930, and then the Red Wings, in 1932. His coach throughout those years was Jack Adams, leading light of the Vancouver team that Noble and his fellow St. Patricks had defeated in the battle for the Stanley Cup back in 1922.

In 1932, in his sixteenth NHL season, Noble was moved one final time, traded back to the Montreal Maroons. He was clearly not the player featured in the hockey cards eight years earlier. In twenty games with Montreal, he tallied no goals, no assists, and no points. At age thirty-six, Noble was finished, the last player from the inaugural 1917 season to play in the NHL.

The damaged right foot continued to serve him well enough in NHL rinks: he stayed in the game as a referee for the 1937–38 and '38–39 seasons.

Reg Noble was another of the former soldiers inducted in the Hockey Hall of Fame in 1962, but the three-time Stanley Cup champion never knew it. He had died at age sixty-five in January that same year, in Alliston, Simcoe County, about an hour south of his boyhood home in Collingwood.

Shorty Green

Passchendaele Survivor

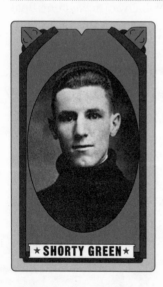

★ SHORTY GREEN ★

227th Battalion/
Canadian Machine Gun Corps (1916–18)

Sudbury Wolves/
Hamilton Tigers/
New York Americans (1919–27)

Hockey Hall of Fame (1962)

★ ★ ★

On July 17, 1896—just six days after Wilfrid Laurier began his fifteen-year run as Canada's seventh prime minister— Wilfrid Thomas Green was welcomed into the world in Sudbury, Ontario.

Young Wilfrid would eventually be far better known as Shorty, though at five feet, seven and a quarter inches in his early manhood he was not especially diminutive by the demographics of his day.

Short or not, Green first made a name for himself as a hockey player in his home town. At age eighteen in 1914, he played the first of two seasons with the amateur Sudbury All-Stars, scoring nineteen goals in a dozen games during his first year.

On April 3, 1916, Green volunteered for overseas service in the Canadian Expeditionary Force (CEF). He enlisted at North Bay in the 227th (Sudbury-Manitoulin-Algoma) Battalion—"The Men o' the North." As he was studying mining engineering at the time, he listed his "trade or calling" as *student*.

One of his early assignments in the CEF was to play hockey for the 227th Battalion in the senior division of the OHA. In 1916–17, he was prolific in a 227th hockey sweater, scoring seventeen goals in just eight games for his battalion team. But the principal duty of the men of the 227th was to fight as soldiers, not play hockey. The 227th departed Canada aboard the SS *Carpathia* in early April 1917 and arrived in England April 22.

Like so many other infantry battalions, the 227th would be disappointed in its expectation of fighting together in the battlefields of Belgium and France. The battalion was ultimately melded into the 8th Reserve Battalion, and its men used to reinforce front-line units decimated by the wastage of war.

Green and his fellow soldiers would spend months in England, training and undergoing medical and dental examinations. One of the forms in Green's service record reflects the attending physician's duty to list identifying "marks, scars or deformities." What stood out for the doctor was Green's broken nose, a 1914 hockey injury. He underwent minor surgery in England to relieve breathing problems resulting from that injury.

On May 17, still in England, he was promoted to acting lance-sergeant, but just two days later he reverted to private, because that was the fastest way to get to the front lines. On May 29, he crossed the English Channel. By late October he was in Belgium, facing all the action he might have imagined he wanted to experience. On October 26, the Canada Corps took its turn in the horrific Third Battle of Ypres—better known as Passchendaele. Serving in the

Shorty Green/Hamilton
Tigers. 1924 V145-2
William Patterson series

Canadian Machine Gun Corps, Private Wilfrid Green became a casualty of war.

On November 6, 1917, some 712 Canadians died at Passchendaele. Private Green survived that day, but he was hospitalized as a result of inhaling German poison gas. Still in hospital a month later, he developed diphtheria and gastritis, no doubt related to his exposure to the gas.

In August 1918, nine months after Passchendaele, Green was still suffering from health problems. A medical case sheet reports him as complaining of shortness of breath—"probably due to gas"—and tachycardia, an irregular heart rhythm. The effects lingered: on November 20, 1918, eight days after the Armistice and more than a year after the Passchendaele gas attack, Green was examined in Seaford, England. He was still far from whole. A medical report described fainting spells, palpitations, fatigue, and anemia. He "does not look strong," the attending physician summarized.

Green was discharged and returned to Canada, arriving at Halifax aboard the SS *Olympic* on December 14.

Back on his home side of the Atlantic, Green's strength was gradually restored. He made his way from Halifax to Hamilton, Ontario, and resumed his hockey career with the amateur OHA Hamilton Tigers. Playing right wing in the 1918–19 season, Shorty Green scored twelve goals in eight games. The Tigers were the eastern representative in that year's Allan Cup playoff, a two-game, total-goal affair. They manhandled the Winnipeg Selkirks 6–1 in the first game but then perhaps grew complacent. The Selkirks stormed back in Game 2, winning 5–1, but Hamilton had managed to hold on and took the Allan Cup by a single goal, 7–6.

The following year, 1919–20, Green was back in Sudbury, playing for another OHA senior club, the Wolves—and playing very effectively. He netted twenty-three goals in just six games with the Wolves, a scoring pace of almost four goals a game.

Green played four seasons with the Wolves before deciding that the time might have come for him to play for profit rather than the simple joy of the game. In 1923, he returned to Hamilton to skate as a pro with the NHL Hamilton Tigers, a team established in 1920 when the Quebec Bulldogs were sold to a Hamilton group. He quickly realized a side benefit of going pro: he made his first appearance on a hockey card, number 30 in the 1923 William Patterson series.

The Tigers had not done well in their first four NHL seasons, finishing dead last in their division each time. In Shorty's first season as a Tiger they finished last again. Then, in 1924–25, Hamilton went from worst to first, with nineteen wins, ten losses, and a tie in the thirty-game schedule. One of the Tigers' leading scorers, Shorty had eighteen goals and twenty-seven points in twenty-eight games—far and away his best numbers in Hamilton. The Tigers were on top of the world.

Then their world caved in. Had their unaccustomed success gone to the players' heads? With the NHL playoffs about to begin, the Hamilton Tigers demanded extra money. With Green one of the ringleaders, the Tigers embarked on the first players' strike in NHL history. They lost the showdown. NHL president Frank Calder suspended Hamilton, and it was the Montreal Canadiens rather than Hamilton that squared off against the western champions, Frank Fredrickson's Victoria Cougars, for the 1925 Stanley Cup. Fredrickson and the Cougars prevailed.

Shorty Green's Tigers had overrated their leverage. The NHL folded the franchise and sold the players' contracts to New York interests. There would never again be another NHL team based in Hamilton.

In 1926–27, Green and his Hamilton collaborators were reconstituted as the New York Americans. Green started well: on December 15 he scored the first-ever goal at Madison Square Garden. One of his teammates that season was Bullet Joe Simpson, but their combined efforts were not enough: after their one season in the limelight, the former Tigers reverted to form, finishing fourth and out of the playoffs.

In two years with the Americans, Shorty Green failed to match the brilliance he had shown in Hamilton: he scored just eight times in fifty-three games.

A casualty at Passchendaele in 1917, Green was a casualty again as a New York American. On February 29, 1928, in a game in Chicago against the Blackhawks, he sustained a serious kidney injury. The kidney was removed and last rites were administered to him. As he had done after Passchendaele, Green recovered, but he had played his last hockey game.

He stayed in hockey, though, and took on a new role as coach. In 1927–28, with Green behind the bench, the Americans again finished last in their division—just eleven victories in forty-four games. It was not an outcome warranting an encore performance. Green enjoyed somewhat better success as a coach in the minor pro American Hockey Association (AHA) at Duluth and Tulsa from 1928 to 1932 before returning for one final time to the scene of the 1925 insurrection—Hamilton.

In 1928–29 he coached a reincarnated Hamilton Tigers of the amateur OHA to a worthy 15–7 record. It was Green's swan song: at age thirty-three he was out of hockey.

In 1962, together with Punch Broadbent and Reg Noble, Shorty Green was inducted in the Hockey Hall of Fame. He never knew of the honour. He had departed his life in 1960 where it had begun: he died of cancer in his sixty-fourth year in Sudbury.

George Boucher
A Heart for Hockey

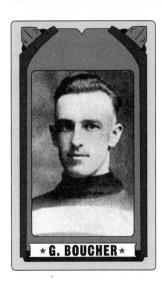

Ottawa Senators/
Montreal Maroons/
Chicago Blackhawks (1915–32)

207th Battalion/
Signal Training Depot (1916–17)

Hockey Hall of Fame (1960)

★ ★ ★

George Boucher of Ottawa was one of six sons of Tom Boucher, a Canadian rugby football star of the 1890s. Four of the brothers would play in the NHL: George, Billy, Frank, and Bobby. Two of them—George and younger brother Frank—were ultimately elected to the Hockey Hall of Fame, one of only six sibling combinations who can boast that distinction.

In addition to hockey, Boucher played three football seasons with the Ottawa Rough Riders of the Canadian Football League, from 1913 to 1915.

In late October 1916, he enlisted at Ottawa in the 207th (Ottawa-Carleton) Battalion, Canadian Expeditionary Force (CEF). He gave his "trade or calling" as *stereotypist*. In 1916, the word meant something other than an individual having a negative opinion of one or more societal sub-groups. Back then a stereotypist was a trade: a worker who made molds for the manufacture of metal printing plates. The medical officer examining Boucher found him fit for overseas service, but for reasons Boucher's war service record does not make clear, he was discharged from the military in December 1916. Evidently keen to do his duty, he completed a second enlistment in May 1917, this time in the Signal Training Depot. Again, the examining physician found him fit for overseas service.

By November 1917, very different medical findings arise in Boucher's service record. The doctors diagnosed Boucher as having "mitral regurgitation," a backward leakage of blood in the heart's mitral valve occurring with each contraction of the left ventricle. With a leaky heart, Boucher was deemed unfit to be a foot soldier in a Canadian infantry battalion. For a reason very different from Reg Noble's disqualification, Boucher was discharged from the CEF—again.

It is rather strange that a CEF volunteer could be rejected as a Canadian infantryman due to a faulty heart but go on to have a seventeen-year career in major league hockey and a place in the Hall of Fame, but that is precisely what would unfold in the life of George "Buck" Boucher.

Boucher began his hockey career in 1913 at age seventeen. Between 1913 and 1917, he played as an amateur in Ottawa—with the New Edinburghs and Royal Canadians—and in Montreal—with La Casquette.

He turned professional with Ottawa in 1915 when the Senators were still in the NHA, the NHL's predecessor. One of George's teammates his first year in Ottawa was Punch Broadbent, the team's scoring leader in George's rookie campaign. Boucher played on the forward line, as left wing, in his first three years with the Senators before switching to defence in 1920–21. His best season as a scorer was his sophomore year, with ten goals in nineteen games.

By 1917–18, Boucher's third year with the Senators, Ottawa was a charter member of the new NHL.

Boucher would win the Stanley Cup four times during his thirteen-year run with his hometown club. The first Cup win came in 1920 when Ottawa defeated the western champions, the Seattle Metropolitans.

After Ottawa took the first two games of the best-of-three series, Flash Foyston's Metropolitans tied the series at two games apiece. In the final game—all five were played at Toronto's Mutual Street Arena—Ottawa won decisively, 6–1. Having scored two goals in the series, Boucher could claim fairly that he had done his bit to make the Senators Stanley Cup champions.

Ottawa repeated its success in 1920–21, this time defeating the Vancouver Millionaires three games to two in a five-game series. All five games were played at Vancouver's Denman Street Arena. Boucher again contributed two goals to the Ottawa scoring parade.

After a year in the Stanley Cup wilderness, the Senators were back in 1923, this time pitted against Duke Keats's Edmonton Eskimos. The Senators scored only three times in a best-of-three series, but those three times were enough to give Ottawa the victory in straight games. Boucher assisted in one of the three Ottawa goals and claimed his third Stanley Cup.

There would be no repeat Stanley Cup in 1924, but Boucher could take satisfaction from two personal successes: leading the NHL in assists that year with ten in twenty-one games, and making his first appearance on a hockey card, number 6 in the 1923 William Patterson series.

George Boucher claimed his fourth and final Stanley Cup victory in 1927. It was the first time the Cup final had been an exclusively NHL affair. The final series against Boston went to four games, two of which were ties. On April 13, 1927, on their home ice—the Ottawa Auditorium—the Senators won the final game, 3–1, but it was not an event any mother would have wanted her son to be a part of.

When Ottawa took a 3–0 lead in the third period, the game descended into a donnybrook. Boucher and the Bruins' Lionel Hitchman squared off as if they were in a boxing ring at Madison Square Garden. The Ottawa police had to intervene to stop the mayhem, and both Hitchman and Boucher were ejected. At the end of the game, Boston's Billy Coutu violently attacked the referee. He would never play another NHL game: Coutu was banned for life.

It was a last time for Boucher too. He would not win another Stanley Cup. In 1928, he was traded to the Montreal Maroons, where he teamed with Red Dutton, a war veteran and future Hall-of-Famer who had nearly lost a leg at Vimy Ridge in 1917. In 1930–31, Boucher played one final year in Montreal but had no scoring points in thirty games.

Jettisoned by the Maroons, Boucher was signed by the Chicago Blackhawks in 1931. In Chicago, he collected just one goal and five assists in forty-three games. At age thirty-six, he called it quits.

Boucher had coached in Montreal for part of the 1930–31 season, and it was to coaching that he now turned for hockey gratification. He returned to Ottawa to coach the Senators in '33–34, and then went to St. Louis to coach the Eagles in their sole NHL season, '34–35. For several years thereafter, he was a coach in minor pro hockey.

In 1949, he coached the now-amateur Ottawa Senators to an Allan Cup victory. The following year, 1949–50, Boucher took one final turn as an NHL coach—with the same club against which he had fought a pitched battle in 1927, the Boston Bruins. With Boucher behind the bench, the Bruins finished second-last.

In 1917, George Boucher may have been rejected for service in the Canada Corps due to a faulty heart but his problematic pump proved up to the task of enabling him to play seventeen seasons in the NHA and NHL. In 1960, he was inducted in the Hockey Hall of Fame—just three weeks before he died from throat cancer in Ottawa at the age of sixty-four.

Bill Cook

From Russia to the Big Apple, with Flair

★ BILL COOK ★

Canadian Field Artillery (1916–19)

Saskatoon Crescents/ New York Rangers (1924–37)

Hockey Hall of Fame (1952)

★ ★ ★

William Osser Xavier (Bill) Cook was born in early October 1896 in Brantford, Ontario, where Alexander Graham Bell had invented the telephone in 1876. He was the eldest of his parents' three sons, all of whom would become hockey players in the NHL. The Cooks moved to Kingston in Bill's tender years and it was there, on the Rideau Canal, that Bill learned to skate.

Bill Cook began building his hockey résumé with the amateur Kingston Frontenacs in 1913, when he was seventeen. In 1915, he set aside his hockey ambitions in order to do his bit for Canada in the Great War.

Cook volunteered for the Canadian Expeditionary Force in early December 1915, enlisting at Kingston in the 50th Battery, Canadian Field Artillery. He gave his "trade or calling" as *student* and his father as next-of-kin. As tens of thousands of other underage volunteers were doing, Cook fibbed about his age. He claimed to be twenty but was actually nineteen.

He embarked for England on April 2, 1916, aboard the SS *Metagama* and landed at Plymouth ten days later. As was usual for soldiers, there followed a period of several months' training and drill in England.

Soldiers typically grew weary of all the training and waiting they had to endure in England. One method of hastening passage to the war zone was to revert to a lower rank, as soldiers in the lower ranks were most in demand on the front lines. The hard truth was that they were needed to replace those killed and wounded in action. Cook had been promoted to acting bombardier, but shortly afterward he reverted to gunner, the lowest artillery rank. In mid-July 1916, he landed in France.

Apart from the occasional interruption caused by non-mortal medical issues, he carried out his artillery duties without becoming a casualty of war. In September 1918, he was restored to his previous rank, acting bombardier.

Meanwhile, with the Russian Revolution now underway, the Canadian government decided to join its allies in sending an expeditionary force to Siberia to help support the Russian government, oppose the Bolsheviks, and keep Russia in the war against Germany. Canada sent more than four thousand troops to Siberia. One of them was Acting Bombardier William O. Cook. In late September 1918, the men of Cook's brigade boarded the troopship *Stephen* for the journey to Siberia. The *Stephen* arrived at Archangel on October 16.

Cook and his comrades were in Russia for eight months. He distinguished himself well enough that in April 1919 he was awarded the Military Medal "in recognition of gallant conduct in the field."

The Russian adventure proved less successful than its British planners had hoped, and in the spring of 1919 the decision was made to

Bill Cook/
Sault Ste. Marie Greyhounds

withdraw the British and Canadian forces. Cook was aboard the troop-ship *Czaritza* when it embarked for England on June 11, 1919. Soon after, on July 5, he was on his way home to Canada. Later that month he was discharged from duty where it had begun three and a half years earlier, Kingston.

Cook picked up where he had left off four years earlier. He rejoined the Kingston Frontenacs in 1919–20 and then migrated more than six hundred miles west to skate for the Sault Ste. Marie Greyhounds of the Northern Ontario Hockey Association in the '20–21 and '21–22 seasons.

In 1922, now aged twenty-six, Cook decided to follow a growing trend: he turned professional. He went west again to join the Saskatoon club of the Western Canada Hockey League. Saskatoon's WCHL team was called the Sheiks, but someone perhaps decided that Sheiks was a moniker more evocative of Arabian desert sands than the snow-covered Saskatchewan prairie, and after one season the Sheiks became the Crescents.

Cook thrived on the banks of the South Saskatchewan River. After a strong—but not stellar—rookie year, he soared in 1923–24. In thirty games with the Crescents, he tallied twenty-six goals and fourteen assists for forty points—six points ahead of a field that included Duke Keats and Dick Irvin.

In 1924, Cook acquired a new teammate, his brother Frederick Joseph—better known as Bun. Bun, younger than Bill by seven years, had been too young to join his brother in the Canada Corps during the war years.

In 1924–25, Cook missed sharing a second scoring title by a single point. The following year, he eclipsed his previous best scoring numbers, registering thirty-one goals and forty-four points in thirty games—but he again missed a share of the league scoring title by a single point.

Cook was a first- or second-team All-Star in each of his Crescent seasons. In 1924, he had additional verification of his hockey stardom: he was featured in the Paulin's Candy Famous Hockey Players hockey card series. His was card number 35.

The western league had suffered from financial problems for some time by this point, and after the conclusion of the 1925–26 season it wound up its affairs. The Cook brothers, together with a raft of other western-league players, had to look elsewhere for hockey employment. The Cooks were courted by the Montreal Maroons, but it was Conn Smythe, manager of a brand-new NHL operation—the New York Rangers—who won the bidding war. Bill and Bun signed with Smythe's Rangers.

It was good for everyone. Named the Rangers' first-ever captain, Bill Cook scored the first-ever Rangers goal. He went on to score thirty-three goals in the New Yorkers' inaugural season, eight better than the league's second-best goal-scorer, Howie Morenz.

In eleven seasons in the Big Apple, Bill Cook would be a first- or second-team All-Star four times. With Bun and George Boucher's brother Frank, Bill formed the famous and formidable Bread Line. Each of the three would eventually have a place in the Hockey Hall of Fame.

Bill Cook was the NHL goal-scoring leader three times, and in 1932–33, he won another overall scoring title with fifty points in forty-eight games. Remarkably, he was thirty-six at the time—the oldest scoring leader in league history.

He had two other star turns in his résumé: he led the Rangers to Stanley Cup championships in 1927 and again in 1933.

Bill Cook played his final shift with the Rangers in 1936–37 at age forty. By then, his scoring numbers had plummeted from those recorded in his heyday—just one goal and four assists in twenty-one games—and he decided it was finally time to call it quits. Over the course of his fifteen-year pro career, Cook had scored 317 goals in 591 regular-season games.

After he quit playing, he turned to coaching and had several stints as a coach in minor pro and amateur hockey between 1937 and 1951. Then, in 1951, he returned to the place where he had enjoyed his finest hours: New York. Cook was behind the Rangers bench for two seasons, neither of which turned out to be as glorious as his best years as a Rangers player: New York finished second-last in 1951–52 and last in '52–53. He would not be an NHL coach again.

Bill Cook was inducted in the Hockey Hall of Fame in 1952, along with Moose Goheen. Bun's turn came forty-three years later, in 1995.

Cook lived a long life. He died in Kingston in his ninetieth year in May 1986. Bun died two years later, also in Kingston, in his eighty-fifth year. Together in hockey, together in the Hall of Fame, they remain together today, buried beside each other in St. Mary's Catholic Cemetery, Kingston.

Red Dutton's

Leg Up

★ RED DUTTON ★

Princess Patricia's Canadian Light Infantry (1917)

**Calgary Tigers/
Montreal Maroons/
New York Americans** (1921–36)

Hockey Hall of Fame (1958)

★ ★ ★

R ussell, Manitoba, is an unincorporated community in the southwestern corner of the province, about nine miles from the Saskatchewan line. Its population today is about sixteen hundred, three times the number in 1914 when its young men began marching off to war. At the junction of Assiniboine Street and Memorial Avenue in Russell there is a war memorial that is remarkable for the presence at its top of a granite soldier standing at the battlefield grave of a fallen comrade. The figure, by Canadian sculptor Emanuel Hahn, is one of the most evocative and compelling you will find anywhere in Canada.

Russell, MB, War Memorial

It takes a while to count all the fallen listed on the Russell monument. Given that Russell's population was only six hundred or so when hostilities erupted in 1914, it is perhaps more than a little remarkable that eighty-two men and one woman—a nurse—are honoured for "giving up their own lives that others might live in freedom." That is a remarkable percentage of the population.

Here is a reliable rule of thumb: for every soldier killed outright in the battlefields of Flanders and France during the Great War of 1914–18, another three were wounded or maimed in body or mind. None of those who were merely wounded or maimed are named on the Russell monument, but a single case study will shed light on the price the wounded also paid for doing their duty.

On May 14, 1915, a young man named Mervyn Dutton enlisted in the Canadian Expeditionary Force at Winnipeg. In the answer to the question "What is your trade or calling?" he wrote "Student." He was enrolled in the University of Manitoba Canadian Officers' Training Corps. Dutton gave his birthdate as July 4, 1897, but then thought better of it. Under the established rules of the CEF, no person under the age of nineteen was permitted to bleed and die for Canada. Dutton therefore saw to it that 1897 was scratched out and replaced with 1896. In the spring of 1915, Dutton stood just short of six feet tall and had blue eyes and—a detail to remember—auburn hair.

Young Mervyn Dutton's lie was not at all remarkable: tens of thousands of Canadian boys misrepresented their age in order not to be blocked from taking their glorious part in the great adventure unfolding in Flanders and France. Dutton went off to war.

Nearly two years later, on a snowy Easter Monday, April 9, 1917, Dutton found himself huddled with comrades in a tunnel below a local northern French promontory called Vimy Ridge. It was 0430 hours, the men of Princess Patricia's Canadian Light Infantry were given a tot of rum to boost any flagging spirits, and then, at an officer's whistled signal, the men of the PPCLI went into action against the German enemy massed on Vimy Ridge. Over the course of the next three days, the Canada Corps would realize its collective objective: it would take Vimy Ridge. The cost included the loss of more than 3,200 men. The PPCLI alone lost eighty men, and nearly twice as many were wounded.

Among the wounded was Mervyn Dutton, his true age then nineteen. The young soldier's wounds were extensive: gunshot wounds to his left leg and buttock and to his right thigh. The military doctors discussed the possibility of amputating his leg. Dutton was fortunate: he was conscious and heard the discussion. He would have none of it. Perhaps he realized sooner than the young soldier of Eric Bogle's *And the Band Played Waltzing Matilda* that "there were worse things than dying." Regardless of the dangers posed by infection or gangrene, Dutton insisted on keeping his leg.

It took seventeen months to restore some semblance of what he and his leg had been before Vimy Ridge. A medical report dated March

1919—nearly two years after Vimy—described a six and a half inch scar on his buttock and indicated that the wounded soldier could now walk up to five miles before having to quit due to pain. Dutton persevered. His fighting days were over, but he had kept his leg. He was discharged at the end of March 1919.

Dutton had been an amateur hockey player of some renown prior to the war. In 1919, he returned to hockey, at first perhaps a bit shakily on a wounded leg but his perseverance and determination prevailed. Back in Winnipeg he flourished in skates, on ice.

In 1921, he turned professional, joining the Calgary Tigers of the WCHL, and at some point acquired the nickname Red, on account of his hair colour. He was named a WCHL All-Star in both 1922 and 1923. After five seasons in Calgary, Dutton joined the Montreal Maroons of the NHL. Skating on the leg he wouldn't allow the army doctors to remove, he shone for ten seasons in the NHL, first with the Maroons and then for six seasons with the New York Americans.

After his experiences at the Western Front, perhaps there wasn't much that intimidated Red Dutton. As a hockey player he was combative, unafraid of confrontation. Three times he led the league in penalty minutes. When his playing days were done, he coached the Americans for five seasons and then became the NHL's second president in 1943. As if that were not enough, he was also trustee of the Stanley Cup for thirty-seven years, from 1950 to 1987.

But for a small bit of serendipity, the world at large would never have heard of Red Dutton. The young soldier had the good fortune to be conscious at the casualty clearing station near Vimy and so overheard the army doctors discussing the necessity of removing his shattered leg. Had he been unconscious—as so many seriously wounded men were— he would have awoken with the shattered leg gone. Dutton would never have been an All-Star pro hockey player, would never have played ten seasons in the National Hockey League, would never have been an NHL president.

Red Dutton/
New York Americans

As it turned out, war was not done with Dutton. When the Second World War broke out in 1939, two of his sons did as he had done—they enlisted. Red Dutton had escaped becoming a name on a Canadian war memorial. His sons did not: both Joseph and Alex died while serving in the Royal Canadian Air Force.

Dutton was inducted in the Hockey Hall of Fame in 1958, together with ten other players featured in this book. He had a good long time to savour the honour. Member of the Order of Canada, Hockey Hall-of-Famer, soldier of the Great War, he died in 1987, seventy years after Vimy, four months short of his ninetieth birthday.

George Hay

The Western Wizard

1960–61 Topps All-Time Greats

101st Battalion/
Canadian Army Service Corps (1916–19)

Regina Capitals/
Portland Rosebuds/
Chicago Blackhawks/
Detroit Cougars (1921–34)

Hockey Hall of Fame (1958)

★ ★ ★

A native of Listowel, Ontario, George Hay moved with his parents to Winnipeg in his early childhood. Hay's career in organized hockey began at age eighteen in 1914, when he played with the amateur Winnipeg Strathconas, and continued with the Winnipeg Monarchs the following year.

One of Hay's teammates in Winnipeg was his boyhood pal Dick Irvin, who was conscripted into the Canadian Expeditionary Force late in the war. Hay did not have to be conscripted. On January 10, 1916, he enlisted in the 101st Battalion (Winnipeg Light Infantry). He was eighteen at the time, but he inflated his age by a year, no doubt feeling confident that the white lie would get him to the Western Front faster than the truth would. In his soldier's attestation, he gave his "trade or calling" as *clerk* and listed as next-of-kin his mother, Louise, of Winnipeg.

While Irvin continued to play hockey, Hay went off to war. After initial training in Canada, he arrived in England aboard the SS *Olympic* on July 6, 1916. He underwent more training and drill at the big British military base at Shorncliffe in Kent. Finally, on September 2, he landed at Le Havre on the French coast.

The 101st Battalion did not endure to fight in the front lines of the Belgian and French battlefields; it was broken up in July, and Hay was transferred first to the 17th Infantry Reserve Battalion and then to the Canadian Army Service Corps.

His medical record indicates no war wounds, but Hay was hospitalized in the summer of 1918 for influenza. This was no minor matter. Millions perished in the 1918–19 Spanish flu pandemic—as many as or more than the number who died as a direct consequence of the war.

For most of the men in the Canada Corps, the November Armistice did not guarantee an early return to Canada. With so many men to move, it could be months before soldiers found themselves on a ship bound for home. Much of the waiting occurred where it did for Hay, at Witley Camp in Surrey. Eventually, rioting and insurrection broke out among the frustrated, aggravated Canadian ranks. Hay, however, was not the rioter sort—he waited. Finally, on April 30, 1919, he embarked for Canada.

Back in his native land, Hay went to Regina in late 1919 to play hockey with the amateur Regina Victorias of the Saskatchewan Senior Hockey League (SSHL). His old friend Dick Irvin was likely instrumental in getting him there: they were teammates on the 1919–20 Victorias. Given that he had been out of hockey for three years, it is no surprise that Hay's scoring numbers were not as glorious as Irvin's: only eight goals as against Irvin's thirty-two.

The friends played together for another season with the Victorias, and then, in 1921–22, they turned pro with the Regina Capitals of the newly established WCHL. This time Hay's scoring figures were the equal of his long-time cohort—both scored twenty-one goals for the Capitals in their inaugural WCHL season.

Hay spent four seasons with the Regina WCHL club, all of them with Dick Irvin skating beside him. His best year was his second in Regina, when he scored twenty-eight goals in thirty games; Irvin scored nine. Hay was a WCHL first-team All-Star three straight years—1922 to 1924.

With the Capitals bleeding money in Regina, the franchise was sold to a Portland, Oregon, group for the 1926–27 season. There in the City of Roses the Capitals morphed into the Rosebuds to play one last campaign before the western league folded for good. Hay enjoyed a productive year—nineteen goals in thirty games—but Irvin performed even better with thirty-one.

Hay acquired a nickname in the Regina years—The Western Wizard—in tribute to his stickhandling and scoring genius. In 1923, there was another indication that he had made the big time: he was included, with Irvin, in the Paulin's Candy hockey card series, Famous Hockey Players.

They had been steadfast teammates at Winnipeg, Regina, and Portland for years, and in 1926–27, they would partner again, this time with a new NHL franchise, the Chicago Blackhawks. A man who had made his fortune in the coffee industry, the Chicago owner was Major Frederick McLaughlin. McLaughlin purchased the Rosebuds franchise to stock his new NHL club.

Like Conn Smythe in Toronto, McLaughlin chose a name and emblem for his hockey team that honoured a military unit he had been associated with during the war, the U.S. 86th Infantry Division—also known as the Blackhawk Division.

In Chicago's inaugural season, the Blackhawks' leading lights were Irvin, Hay, and a player named Babe Dye. Hay scored the first-ever

Blackhawks goal, against Toronto, on November 26, 1926. Over the course of the whole season, Dye was the scoring leader with twenty-five goals. Irvin potted eighteen, Hay fourteen.

Finally, after eight years together, Hay and Irvin parted ways in 1927. But not by choice. In April 1927, McLaughlin dealt The Western Wizard to the Detroit Cougars for a player and cash.

The 1927–28 Detroit roster included Frank Foyston, Duke Keats, and Reg Noble. Hay did well in his first Detroit campaign, recording twenty-two goals and thirty-five points in forty-two games to lead them all.

In Detroit, Hay found a place to call his final hockey home. He spent his remaining six years as a player in the Motor City, long enough to wear the emblem of all three Detroit identities—Cougars, Falcons, and Red Wings. Hay's coach in every one of those seasons was Jack Adams.

Adams once described George Hay as among his most willing, agreeable, and easy-to-handle players. In 1928, Hay was runner-up to the Rangers' Frank Boucher in voting for the award presented annually to the league's most gentlemanly player—the Lady Byng Trophy.

Hay's best Detroit season was 1929–30. With eighteen goals and fifteen assists in forty-four games, he fell just three points shy of the team's leading scorer. There followed three seasons of decline: his goal totals fell to eight, one, and then none. In 1934, at the age of thirty-six, Hay put away his skates.

He turned to minor league coaching for a few years before retiring in 1939, just as another world war was unfolding in Europe. In 1958, he was among the big group of players featured in this book who were inducted in the Hockey Hall of Fame. Hay had several years to enjoy the honour. He died at Stratford, Ontario, about forty minutes south of Listowel, where he had taken his first breath seventy-seven years before.

Babe Dye

Athlete of Many Parts

69th Battery, Canadian Field Artillery (1918)

Toronto St. Patricks/
Chicago Blackhawks/
New York Americans (1919–29)

Hockey Hall of Fame (1970)

★ ★ ★

Cecil Henry "Babe" Dye was eighteen when he launched his career in organized hockey with the amateur Toronto Aura Lee club in 1916. In the 1916–17 season, he scored a fairly astounding thirty-one goals in just eight games. A Canadian Hobey Baker of sorts, Dye was a talented practitioner of several sports. An accomplished halfback with the Toronto Argonauts football team from 1917 to 1920, he was an even better baseball player.

For a period of several years Dye was a multitasker: he played hockey in winter, baseball in summer. He shone in both sports. He played baseball for the Buffalo Bisons of the International League, a rung below baseball's major leagues. Between 1922 and 1925, he had a batting average above .300 three times in his four summers as a Bisons outfielder—and just missed a fourth. He would also play for Baltimore and Toronto of the International League before deciding in 1926 to focus on hockey.

A baseball player of some renown, George Herman Ruth had acquired the nickname Babe back in 1914. It seems that some of Dye's hockey teammates felt that if the moniker was good enough for Mr. Ruth, it was good enough for Dye too: Cecil became Babe.

Before all that, however, there had been a brief interruption in Babe Dye's sporting career. He was a late volunteer in the Canadian Expeditionary Force (CEF), enlisting in Toronto on May 3, 1918, in the 69th Battery, Canadian Field Artillery. On that date, Dye was ten days short of his twentieth birthday. He gave his "trade or calling" as *clerk* and his mother, Esther, as next-of-kin.

The service record suggests that Dye spent much of the ensuing months at the Petawawa training camp on the Ottawa River, about a hundred miles west of the nation's capital. The war ended six months after his enlistment—too soon for him to have been properly trained to do battle as a gunner in the Canadian Artillery. And too soon for him to have been shipped across the Atlantic to battle the Kaiser's armies.

Nothing in his service record suggests that Dye presented his commanders with any medical or disciplinary issues. The most intriguing item in the record is an official form dated July 31, 1918, in which his mother, Esther, pleads poverty and seeks an allowance in recognition of her son's military service. In her application, Esther Dye reports having been abandoned by Dye's father in 1898—the year of Dye's birth. The service record ends with this document. There is no indication of whether Mrs. Dye's application succeeded.

Discharged from the CEF in December, Dye had time to lace up for the amateur Toronto St. Patricks in 1918–19. He scored thirteen goals in nine games with the St. Pats. In '20–21, the St. Patricks joined the NHL, then in its fourth year. The demands of pro hockey seemed not to trouble Dye in the least: he scored thirty-five goals in twenty-three games. That total bettered not only his teammate Reg Noble's total—by sixteen goals—but also that of every other player in the entire NHL.

The following year, Dye enjoyed another banner season, with thirty-one goals, but finished third in the scoring race behind the Ottawa Senators' goal-scoring machine, Punch Broadbent. But there was compensation: it was Toronto, not Ottawa, that reached the Stanley Cup final in 1922. The St. Pats prevailed over the Vancouver Millionaires, and Babe Dye's name was inscribed on hockey's Holy Grail. It would turn out to be Dye's only Cup victory.

Dye flourished in Toronto for six years. In 1922, after batting .312 with the baseball Bisons, he switched his baseball cleats for hockey skates and accumulated thirty-seven points in twenty-two games for the St. Pats—the best in the NHL that 1922–23 season.

If they had doubted it before, hockey-loving boys understood by 1923 that Babe Dye was a bona fide hockey star: that year, his card was number 23 in the William Patterson series.

In 1923, Dye upped his baseball batting average to .318 and smacked sixteen home runs to boot. In the subsequent hockey season he missed a third straight NHL scoring title by a single point. That must have displeased him. In the following summer of 1924, with Buffalo, Dye had another solid year: more than two hundred base hits and a batting average of .311. Now in his prime at age twenty-six, Dye proceeded to surpass himself: he scored a career high of thirty-eight goals in the 1924–25 NHL season and won another NHL scoring title.

In 1925–26, Babe Dye slipped a little—eighteen goals in thirty-one games—and fell out of the list of the NHL's top ten scorers. Did that decline signal that he was past his prime? Toronto management might have imagined so: they shipped their distinguished scorer to the rival Chicago Blackhawks for $15,000 in late October 1926.

The trade may have given Dye extra incentive for the 1926–27 season. Teamed with Dick Irvin and George Hay, he led Chicago with twenty-five goals and finished fourth in the NHL American

Division's scoring race behind Bill Cook, Irvin, and Frank Fredrickson. It must have been sweet for Dye that his scoring numbers were ahead of every one of the '26–27 St. Patricks players'. But his satisfaction would not endure.

In 1927, while preparing for the upcoming NHL season, Dye suffered a broken leg. It healed in time for him to play ten games with the Blackhawks in 1928, but he was never the same again. He scored not a single goal in those ten games. On October 17, 1928, he was sold to the New York Americans for the same money he had commanded two years earlier: $15,000.

Dye's single season in New York was no better than his previous one in Chicago: he scored just one goal in forty-two games. He was then sold to a minor league team in New Haven, where he managed eleven goals in thirty-four games. That was perhaps barely enough to entice his former club—now named the Toronto Maple Leafs—to give him another shot in the NHL. It did not end well: Dye played just six games with the Leafs without scoring a goal. His playing career was over at the age of thirty-two.

He turned to coaching. First, for the OHA Port Colborne Sailors and then for the Shamrocks of the AHA in Chicago. The Shamrocks did well with Dye behind the bench but he was fired over a personnel decision his bosses didn't like.

Despite the unhappy ending in Chicago, Dye decided to remain there. For many years he worked for an oil company. In 1962, he suffered a major heart attack that put him in hospital for an extended period. He died at age sixty-three on January 3, 1962.

Eight years later, in 1970, Babe Dye was posthumously inducted in the Hockey Hall of Fame, the last of the Great War soldier-players to be accorded that distinction. There would be another honour that came too late to give him any satisfaction: in 1998 the game's "bible," *The Hockey News*, included Babe Dye in its list of the best one hundred players of all time.

Harry Ellis Watson
Three Kinds of Unique

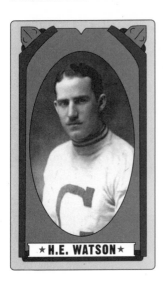

Royal Flying Corps (1916–18)

**Toronto Granites/
Canadian Olympic Team** (1919–24)

Hockey Hall of Fame (1962)

★ ★ ★

Only one player in the Hockey Hall of Fame was a native Newfoundlander, only one was a fighter pilot ace in the Great War, and only one skated to a gold medal for Canada in the 1924 Olympics. In the summer of 1898, a time when Newfoundland was a separate British Dominion—not part of Canada—Harry Ellis Watson was born in St. John's. By his mid-teens he had lived in England and Winnipeg. He then moved to Toronto as a fifteen-year-old in 1913.

That same year, young Watson made his organized hockey debut with the amateur Whitby Athletics of the OHA junior division. A year later, he was a first-team All-Star with the OHA's Toronto St. Andrew's club. In 1915, he began a two-year term with the Toronto Aura Lee club. In the second season, 1916–17, Watson teamed with Babe Dye to lead Aura Lee to an undefeated campaign in its OHA junior division. Watson, Dye, and company won all six of their regular-schedule games, outscoring the opposition 60–13.

In early 1917, Watson parted ways from Dye in order to go to war. The Newfoundland Regiment, an infantry battalion, had come to catastrophic grief at Beaumont-Hamel on the Somme on July 1, 1916. Watson decided that he would fight the war not as a foot soldier but as an airman in the King's Royal Flying Corps (RFC).

He completed his air training and in early 1918 was attached to RFC No. 41 Squadron based at Saint-Omer in northern France. With 41 Squadron, Lieutenant Watson flew the Royal Aircraft Factory SE5A, a newish, highly regarded machine that pilots loved and that had helped turn the war in the air in the allies' favour in 1917.

On January 25, 1918, Lieutenant Watson claimed his first air victory over an enemy flier piloting an Albatros D.V. It was a victory shared with a fellow pilot from 41 Squadron. Two months later, on March 21, the first day of spring, Watson downed a Fokker DR.I in the skies over Bourlon Wood. It was his second victory, and one entirely his own.

June 30 was a red-letter day for Watson. On that day he downed two enemy machines in the vicinity of Bray, each of them a Pfalz D.III. In quick succession, in the first week of July, he had two more victories, bringing him to a total of six. Five air victories was the number that qualified a pilot to be counted as a fighter ace.

Though he'd been born in Newfoundland, Watson was a Canadian resident by 1918 when he joined the ranks of 194 Canadians classified as Great War aces—men such as Billy Bishop, Raymond Collishaw, and William Barker.

A good number of those Canadian aces died in the war, but Watson survived and returned to Canada in time to play at least part of the 1918–19 season with the OHA Toronto Dentals. In '19–20, he began a five-year stint with the OHA Toronto Granites—hockey being a sideline of the Toronto Granite Curling Club.

Still only twenty-one after two years in the RFC, Watson shone with the Granites, scoring seventeen goals in eight games. He would improve year by year with the Granites, peaking in 1922–23 with twenty-one goals in twelve games.

The Granites reached the top of the mountain in 1922, winning the Canadian amateur championship—and the Allan Cup—with a two-game 13–2 thrashing of the Regina Victorias.

In 1923, with Coach Frank Rankin now calling the shots from behind the bench, the Granites repeated as Allan Cup champions. This time their victims were the University of Saskatchewan skaters. The U of S players performed little better than Regina's had done a year earlier: they lost to Watson and his collaborators 11–2 in another two-game series. Watson was selected as a first-team All-Star and the OHA's most valuable player in both Allan Cup years.

On the strength of its 1923 Allan Cup win, the Granites qualified themselves to represent Canada at the 1924 Olympic Games at Chamonix, France. The Canadians played fourteen games in the lead-up to the Olympics. Watson had a field day, scoring twenty-four

1924 Canadian Olympic Hockey Team, **Harry Watson**, far left

goals. Once they arrived in Chamonix for the actual Olympic contests, Watson grew even more prolific. In just five games against the other Olympic squads, he scored thirty-six goals.

The Canadians were even more dominant than they had been four years earlier in Antwerp when they had been led by Frank Fredrickson. In the preliminary round, the game scores were remarkable: 30–0 over Czechoslovakia, 22–0 over Sweden, and 33–0 over Switzerland, making an aggregate 85–0 score.

After the routing of Switzerland, the Swiss goaltender—perhaps exaggerating a little—opined that he would as soon have faced a machine gun as the relentless barrage of bruising shots fired by Watson and his relentless crew.

The medal round was almost as one-sided. The Canadians humbled Great Britain 19–2 and then, in the gold medal game, beat the USA 6–1.

It is small wonder that the professional leagues took notice of Watson's performance in Chamonix. In 1925, he was offered a significant sum—said to be $30,000—to turn pro with the Montreal Maroons of the NHL. But Watson was a throwback. Like Phat Wilson, he had no intention of sullying his joy in the game by playing for filthy lucre. He said no thanks to the Maroons.

By 1924 another entrepreneur had decided that getting into the sports card business made good sense. The Willard Chocolate people introduced both baseball and hockey cards that year. Harry Watson was featured on card number 43 in Willard's hockey card series.

Between 1924 and 1932, Watson played another six seasons of amateur hockey in the OHA—with the Parkdale Canoe Club, Toronto Marlboros, and Toronto Nationals—but he did not shine as brightly as he had done at Chamonix. How could he have?

Watson called it quits as a player in 1932 at age thirty-three but stayed in hockey as a coach for a few years. In 1932, he coached the Toronto National Sea Fleas—yes, Sea Fleas—to an Allan Cup title. This qualified the Sea Fleas to represent Canada at the 1933 world hockey championships in Prague, but Watson preferred to stay home—which was perhaps unfortunate for the Canadians. The Americans turned the tables on Canada, winning the gold medal game 2–1. The Canadians had to settle for silver.

Harry Watson never played a shift of professional hockey—he was one of the last of the unshakeable amateurs in the Hall of Fame, where he was admitted in 1962, along with his fellow purist, Phat Wilson. The Hockey Hall of Fame honour materialized a tad late for the ace fighter pilot. Watson had died—too young at age fifty-nine—in Toronto five years earlier.

Ivan the Terrible (Ching) Johnson *Beloved in New York*

★ CHING JOHNSON ★

3rd and 4th Divisional Ammunition Columns, Canadian Expeditionary Force (1916–19)

New York Rangers/ New York Americans (1926–38)

Hockey Hall of Fame (1958)

★ ★ ★

In late 1898, with Wilfrid Laurier in the midst of his first term as Canadian prime minister, Ivan Wilfred Johnson was born in the worst Winnipeg winter in years. The average temperature that December was -4.9°F. Despite the appalling temperatures, mother and child both survived.

Seventeen years after that worst Winnipeg winter, in January 1916, Johnson volunteered for overseas service with the Canadian Expeditionary Force (CEF). He was barely seventeen that winter day, but he claimed to be eighteen. He enlisted in the Third Division Ammunition Column, service number 311977. He listed his "trade or calling" as *student* and his father as next-of-kin.

On March 25, 1916, Johnson arrived in England aboard the SS *Metagama*. After initial training in England, he landed at Le Havre on the French coast in mid-July. During the ensuing months, he underwent additional training and was eventually assigned to the Fourth Division Ammunition Column. Nothing in his service record suggests that anything untoward arose as he played his part in delivering ammunition to front-line battalions and batteries.

In October 1917, he was granted ten days' leave. Some of the diversions he enjoyed while on leave are perhaps suggested by another entry in the service record: on November 5, 1917, as ninety-one men of the Canada Corps were fighting and dying at Passchendaele, Johnson was admitted to No. 44 Casualty Clearing Station, his condition signified by the initials VDG: Venereal Disease, Gonorrhea.

It is unsurprising that the Canada Corps commanders took a dim view of men removed from service as a result of VDG—as a great number of Canadians were during the war. The Canadians' sexually transmitted infection rate—one in nine over the course of the war—was more dreadful than that of the next-worst offenders, the blithesome Australians. It was one thing for a soldier to be hospitalized as a result of gunshot wounds delivered by enemy shell blasts or machine gun bursts, but quite another for a man to be lost due to reckless sexual behaviour.

Johnson's field allowance was forfeited and he was "placed under stoppage of pay" for the time spent in hospital. Doctors described his condition as "acute." It must have been: he was in hospital for eighty-four days.

Studying Johnson's service record, it is a little surprising to see that on June 22, 1918, he was awarded a Good Conduct Badge. What good deeds had he done in four months to erase the stain that had taken him out of action for eighty-four days? His service record offers no illumination. In any event, he managed to avoid becoming any sort of casualty for the rest of the war.

Of course, that did not mean that Private Johnson was on the next homeward-bound ship. The Armistice was already five months in the

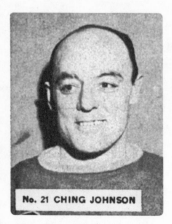

No. 21 CHING JOHNSON

Ching Johnson/New York Rangers.
1936–37 V356 World Wide Gum series

rear-view mirror by the time he was able to depart Le Havre for England. The following month, on May 18, 1919, he embarked from Southampton aboard the SS *Aquitania* and arrived at Halifax a week later. On May 29, he was discharged from the CEF.

Ivan Johnson came relatively late to organized hockey. In 1919–20, at age twenty, he played with the amateur Winnipeg Monarchs—the alma mater of Dick Irvin and George Hay. A year later, he travelled to Eveleth, Minnesota, to play three seasons with the Rangers of the United States Amateur Hockey Association (USAHA). Johnson obviously liked what he saw of Minnesota—Moose Goheen would have understood—as he played three more seasons with Minneapolis teams, the Millers and the Rockets.

In 1926, at the relatively advanced age of twenty-eight, Ivan decided to turn professional. In advance of the 1926–27 season, he signed a contract to play for a new NHL team, the New York Rangers. The Rangers' leading light that inaugural season was Johnson's fellow war veteran, Bill Cook.

Regarded as one of the toughest body-checkers in the game, Johnson was initially dubbed Ivan the Terrible, but that nickname was soon supplanted by another—Ching. One dubious claim is that the name somehow reflected his cooking talent. Really? Another, more credible, explanation is that the name referred to Johnson's Asian-looking appearance. The nickname stuck—cherished not as a racist epithet shouted by zealots supporting opposing teams but by Johnson's own adoring fans. Johnson's mother doubtless preferred that her son be called Ivan.

As a defenceman, Johnson never accumulated big scoring numbers in New York, but no one could touch Ivan the Terrible in another statistical category: in his eleven seasons with the Rangers he led the team in penalty minutes eight times. Perhaps his time in the battlefields of Flanders and France had inured him to violence.

There are markers other than goals and assists that can be drawn on to appreciate Johnson's success as a major league hockey player. In New York, he was a first- or second-team NHL All-Star four straight times, from 1931 to 1934. In 1932, he finished second in the NHL's MVP voting, behind Montreal's great Howie Morenz. He played in the NHL's first All-Star game in 1934, was featured in several hockey card series, and was hugely popular with fans. In 1928 and in 1933 he was a Stanley Cup champion with the Rangers.

By the 1936–37 season, Johnson's All-Star days were clearly behind him. He played thirty-five games with the Rangers without registering a single goal or assist. The Broadway Blueshirts, as the Rangers were known, cut him loose. But there was another team in New York: the Americans. Their management felt that Johnson might sell tickets—and help on the ice at the same time. In his final NHL season, the fan favourite matched his output of the previous years: no goals and no assists in thirty-one games.

At age thirty-eight, Ivan Johnson was not done with hockey, even if the NHL was done with him. He returned to Minnesota to play two seasons with the Minneapolis Millers of the minor pro AHA. In 1938, he returned to Minnesota for two seasons as player-coach with the Millers. In 1944–45, at age forty-six, he worked as on-ice official—a linesman—in the AHA.

In 1943, with another world war raging in Europe, Johnson came back to hockey to take a turn in Hollywood. He played a season with the Hollywood Wolves of the Southern California Hockey League. Playing a season at age forty-six was remarkable enough, but Johnson had one more surprise to offer his fans. In 1953–54, he played one last season, with the Edmonton Flyers of the Western Hockey League (WHL). At age fifty-six, he managed to score five goals in nineteen games. Not even the ageless Gordie Howe played the game so far into his second half-century.

During his best New York years, Johnson was beloved for his talent, skill, and joie de vivre. He was inducted in the Hockey Hall of Fame—as Ching Johnson—in 1958, the same year so many of the

Ching Johnson/New York Rangers

players featured in these pages were honoured. Having started out in life in freezing Winnipeg, Johnson was not tempted to return to Manitoba in his retirement years. He had made his home in a place favoured by Rachel Carson and Carl Bernstein—Silver Spring, Maryland—about six miles due north of Washington, DC, and lived there until his death in 1979.

Alex Connell

One-of-a-Kind Goaltender

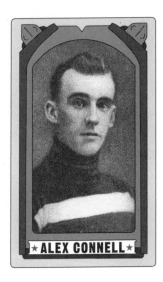

★ ALEX CONNELL ★

Canadian Army Service Corps (1919)

Ottawa Senators/Detroit Falcons/ Montreal Maroons (1924–37)

Hockey Hall of Fame (1958)

★ ★ ★

Alex Connell enlisted at Kingston in the Canadian Expeditionary Force (CEF) in early May 1919, six months after the November 1918 Armistice. There was no longer a war raging in Flanders and France, but Canadian soldiers were still serving in Europe, some as part of the occupation force in Germany, others with the Canadian Siberian Expeditionary Force. The late recruit listed his "trade or calling" as *chauffeur* and named his mother as next-of-kin.

Apart from the wrinkle that the war was essentially over by the spring of 1919, there was another issue with Alex Connell's enlistment. He claimed to have born in February 1899 and was thus twenty years of age on the day he signed his attestation. Alex's mother, Sarah, knew better.

As we have seen repeatedly in this book, it was commonplace for young men keen to play their glorious part in the European adventure to falsify their age. Youths under the age of nineteen were not permitted to enlist, and so many underage recruits misrepresented their age in order to get past recruiting sergeants. In Alex Connell's case, what was delivered was not so much a little fib as a great whopping lie. In the enlistment document, he reported his birthday correctly—February 8—but his birth year was not 1899. It was actually 1902. Connell was barely seventeen the day he enlisted in the CEF.

A standard feature in the CEF attestation form was a section calling on the examining physician to list any "distinctive marks" a soldier presented. Such details could prove useful should it become necessary to identify the body of a soldier killed in action. In Connell's case, the doctor observed that the young recruit's face was "badly scarred" by acid. Perhaps this entry reflected a slip of the pen, as a later examination by a different doctor reiterated that Connell's face was badly scarred but this time the blame was pinned on *acne*, not acid. Connell was, of course, not the only seventeen-year-old having to cope with acne issues.

Whatever his true age, Connell was assigned to the Canadian Army Service Corps, but his military career proved to be very brief. He did not cross the Atlantic to join the Canadians occupying Germany. He did not travel to Archangel to do his bit with the Canadian Siberian Expeditionary Force. He stayed in Kingston. In fact, he barely had time to be fitted for his uniform before he was discharged from the CEF. The discharge process was completed in August 1919. Under "Conduct and Character," Private Connell was rated as having been *good*.

A goaltender, Alex Connell had begun his time in organized hockey at age fourteen with the Kingston Ponies. Over the next several years he would complete his hockey apprenticeship with the Kingston Frontenacs juniors and with several Ottawa clubs—the Cliffsides, St. Brigands, and Gunners.

By 1924, when the playing careers of a number of the players featured in this book were only memories, Alex Connell signed his first professional deal with the Ottawa Senators. He was twenty-two. One of Alex's teammates on the 1924–25 squad was George Boucher, older by five years than the rookie goaltender. Connell sparkled in the Ottawa net with a goals-against average (GAA) of 2.14.

The next year he did even better, dropping his GAA to a remarkable 1.12, with just forty-two goals allowed in thirty-six games. In fifteen of those games, Connell allowed no goals at all. He carried on in the same vein the following year, 1926–27, shutting out the opposition in thirteen of thirty games and recording a GAA of under 1.5 goals a game.

That season was the first in which the contest for the Stanley Cup became an NHL-only affair. In the Stanley Cup playoffs, Connell surpassed himself. In six games, he never allowed more than a single goal. He shut out his Stanley Cup opponents twice and recorded a GAA of 0.60. Connell's Senators won the Stanley Cup, defeating first the Montreal Canadiens and then the Boston Bruins.

Connell's 1927–28 campaign was just as remarkable. As in '25–26, he had fifteen shutouts and a minuscule GAA—1.24 this time. Playing with Boucher and Punch Broadbent in front of Connell, the Senators had a good year—but not as splendid as the Montreal Canadiens'. Montreal beat Connell and company in a best-of-three semi-final, 1–0 and 2–1.

Over the course of three seasons Connell shut out the opposition forty-five times—including twice in the playoffs. Even today, ninety years after his extraordinary early seasons in Ottawa, he is the only goaltender in NHL history to record fifteen shutouts in more than a single regular season. In 1928, from January 31 to February 18, Connell shut out the opposition in six straight games. It is an NHL record that still stands nine decades later.

Connell played another three seasons in Ottawa, and although his performance was good by mortal standards it was not the sublime phenomenon it had been from 1925 through 1928. Ottawa's on-ice performance fell, and so did the team's box office allure. In 1930–31, even with Alex Connell in goal, Ottawa finished dead last in the NHL's Canadian Division. The team management suspended operations and the players were subject to a dispersal draft, distributed to other NHL clubs for that season. Alex Connell was chosen by the Detroit Cougars.

In 1931–32, Connell did well in Detroit. Playing for Jack Adams and alongside a past-his-prime Reg Noble, Connell recorded six more shutouts and had a sparkling 2.12 GAA.

In 1932, the Ottawa franchise was resuscitated, and Connell returned to the scene of his finest years. There was nothing shameful about his GAA—2.56—but the Senators again finished last in the Canadian Division. At age thirty-two, Connell was offloaded to the Montreal Maroons.

Over the course of two seasons in Montreal, Connell revived memories of his best years in Ottawa. In 1934–35, his GAA was 1.86 and he shut out the Maroons' opponents nine times. He had waited eight years, but in 1935, he got to hoist the Stanley Cup a second time. In the playoffs, he was the Alex Connell of old, yielding just eight goals in seven games—a 1.12 GAA. In the Cup final, Montreal swept the Toronto Maple Leafs in three straight games, outscoring the Leafs 10–4.

In the hockey off-season, Alex Connell had a senior position with the Ottawa Fire Department. Unable to arrange time off to play in 1935–36, he did without hockey that season but returned the following year for one final go-round with the Maroons. In '36–37, at age thirty-four, he had a GAA of 2.21 with two shutouts in twenty-seven games. He decided to retire his goaltender pads and devote himself to his fire department duties.

Alex Connell finished his twelve-year hockey career with a GAA of 1.91. That 1.91 average remains the best in NHL history. Connell is one more among the large group of soldier-players admitted to the Hockey Hall of Fame in 1958. He was alive to hear the announcement but did not live long enough to participate in the induction ceremony. He died after a long illness on May 10, 1958, where he had thrilled hockey fans three decades earlier, at Ottawa. He was just fifty-six years old.

— 5 —

AFTERMATH

The impact of the Great War on the game of hockey did not end with the Armistice of November 1918.

F or every man killed in action in Belgium and France, another three were wounded in body or mind. Some wounds healed over time; others endured a lifetime, a lifetime that in many cases lasted only a year or two after the Armistice. Like tens of thousands of other war veterans, the soldier-players inducted in the Hall of Fame—men like Conn Smythe, Red Dutton, and Shorty Green—would have to deal with its consequences for the rest of their days. Some of the wounds were the physical relics of enemy shell blasts or rifle bullets or poison gas. Other wounds, emotional and psychological, were not as readily spotted by the casual observer.

The Great War's legacy endures to this day in the game of hockey. In 1919, a new trophy was established for annual presentation to Canada's national junior hockey champions—the Memorial Cup. It honours the "splendid work done by Canadian boys in France," particularly those who had been hockey players before they died in the battlefields of the Western Front. The inaugural winners of the Memorial Cup in 1919 were the men of the University of Toronto Schools club. In 2017, ninety-eight years later, the Windsor Spitfires of the Ontario Hockey League (OHL) won the Memorial Cup for the third time in ten years.

For nearly four decades starting in 1932, the silverware awarded to the eastern Canadian junior champions was the George Richardson Memorial Trophy. The football home field of the Queen's University Grenadiers is Richardson Stadium.

In the National Hockey League (NHL), the award given annually since 1925 to the player judged as exhibiting the worthiest combination of sportsmanship and skill is the Lady Byng Trophy. Lady Byng was the spouse of Canada's twelfth Governor-General, 1st Viscount Byng of Vimy, who eight years earlier, as Lieutenant-General Julian Byng, led Mervyn Dutton and the Canada Corps to its great victory at Vimy Ridge. The Lady Byng prize was awarded to George Boucher's brother Frank, who had been too young to enlist in the war, nine times.

In the United States, the award given since 1981 to the university hockey player judged to be the best in the National Collegiate Athletic Association is the Hobey Baker Award.

McGee, Davidson, Richardson, and Baker are the best known of the hockey players who have died in active service—and they are the only four to have a place in the Hockey Hall of Fame. But the list of players who fell in war is far greater than four. The Society for International Hockey Research lists more than thirteen hundred hockey players as having done military service in the world wars, including 269 killed in action.

After the Armistice, war would continue to cast a shadow over the game of hockey and the NHL. In 1939, war in Europe erupted again. The Second World War is considered by many historians as Part II of the conflict that had ended just twenty-one years earlier. The major adversaries were the same as in 1914–18: Germany and its allies on one side; Britain, France, and Russia on the other. In both wars, the United States joined the fray later, on the side of Britain and France.

In Part II of the global conflict, young men did as they had done a generation earlier: they sidelined their normal trades and became soldiers. Hockey players followed suit. They set aside their sticks and skates for boots and rifles.

The Second World War had a great impact on the NHL. Almost two hundred players with NHL experience joined the military between

1939 and 1945. Thirty player members of the Hockey Hall of Fame had served in the First World War. Two-thirds as many—twenty-one Hall-of-Famers—did the same in the Second World War.

For two Hall-of-Famers—Conn Smythe and Frank Fredrickson—once was not enough. Having done their duty in Part I, they felt obliged to serve again in Part II.

Though his name arises again and again in this book, Lester Patrick had chosen not to be a soldier in the Great War. He was thirty years old when the guns began to thunder in August 1914, but Lester and his brother Frank were busy establishing their Pacific Coast Hockey Association (PCHA) and building their reputations as perhaps the game's greatest innovators.

Lester's son Lynn, also a member of the Hockey Hall of Fame, was an established NHL star in his ninth season with the New York Rangers when he decided to answer Uncle Sam's call and join the United States' war effort in 1943.

Enlistments by star NHL players were a trial for the operators of the NHL, many of whom were more concerned about the value of their product than about patriotism or service to King and Country.

Despite an ethnic heritage reflected in their famous name—The Kraut Line—three star players of the Boston Bruins, all of them of German extraction, went to war against Adolf Hitler's Nazi Germany: Milt Schmidt, Bobby Bauer, and Woody Dumart. In doing so, each of them would miss four years of their hockey prime. The Boston Bruins would lose something too.

In the 1941–42 season, the Bruins had finished only four points from first place in the NHL's regular season. In '44–45, with Bauer, Dumart, and Schmidt in Europe, the Bruins won only sixteen of fifty scheduled games and finished forty-four points from first place.

Though no one inducted in the Hockey Hall of Fame died in the Second World War, Hall-of-Famers *were* casualties of this war, just as they had been in its predecessor.

Howie Meeker, beloved by *Hockey Night in Canada* fans in a time before Don Cherry took over as its colour commentator, was the NHL rookie of the year at age twenty-three in 1946–47. In 1944, his entry to the NHL was delayed by his decision to fight for Canada in the war. Soldier Meeker was so badly wounded by a grenade blast that he was told he might never walk again—as grim a forecast as Red Dutton had faced a generation before. Meeker confounded the prognosis, won the Calder Trophy as rookie of the year in 1947, went on to play eight seasons with the Toronto Maple Leafs, and was admitted to the Hockey Hall of Fame as a broadcaster in 1998.

A hundred years ago none of the soldier-players treated in this book had any idea that there would one day be a hockey hall of fame, an insti-

1958 Hockey Hall of Fame induction ceremony (photo taken in 1959). Names in **bold** are men who were also soldiers in the Great War.

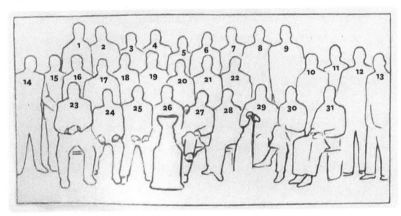

1. Red Dutton; 2. Lloyd Turner; **3. Frank Goheen**; **4. Ching Johnson**; 5. Aurel Joliat; **6. Frank Boucher**; **7. Al Pickard**; 8. Bill Cook; 9. George Hay; 10. Duke Keats; 11. Dit Clapper; 12. Eddie Shore; 13. Conn Smythe; 14. King Clancy; 15. Wm. Northey; **16. Frank Foyston**; 17. George Drudley; **18. Frank Fredrickson**; 19. Lester Patrick; 20. Newsy Lalonde; 21. Frank Nighbor; 22. Joe Malone; 23. Herb Gardiner; 24. W.A. Hewitt; 25. Hugh Lehman; 26. Art Ross; 27. Cyclone Taylor; 28. Dickie Boon; 29. Claude Robinson; 30. Moose Johnson; 31. Paddy Moran

tution in which they would each be accorded an honoured place. On a sunny day in early September 1959 thirty-one Hall-of-Fame hockey players gathered in Toronto to celebrate the induction of the class of 1958. Fully a third of the men of this book were among the 1958 inductees. By 1959 the youngest of the new inductees was sixty years old, the eldest closing in on seventy. Though none look as fit as in their playing prime, they are all recognizable.

Included among the large group are all eight of the 1958 inductees available to attend. Three had an ironclad reason for not being there: they were no longer in the land of the living. Three earlier soldier-player inductees were also on hand for the momentous event, for a total of eleven of the thirty-two Hall-of-Famers addressed in these pages. Take a close look: it is a fascinating old portrait. Four of the soldier-players were of course long gone, men in uniform who had stepped forward to do their duty, men who had paid the ultimate price for doing so.

Throughout the former battlefields of Belgium and northern France there are war cemeteries containing the remains of soldiers who did not survive their wounds. A map book produced by the Commonwealth War Graves Commission plots more than *nine hundred* memorials and cemeteries where soldiers of the First and Second World Wars lie forevermore. Some of the war cemeteries are huge, with as many as ten thousand graves. Others are tiny, with only a few dozen graves. Among the grandest of the monuments mapped in the CWGC guide is the great Canadian memorial to the missing on the summit of Vimy Ridge in France.

The monument lists the names of 11,157 Canadian soldiers who died in the fighting in France in the First World War and have no known grave. No one visiting Vimy could fail to be moved by the manifest consequences of the Great War, not only for young Canadian men but also for Canadian families from one end of the country to the other. The monument somehow manages to be both beautiful and appalling.

It requires a great number of inscribed panels to list eleven thousand names. Two of the names at Vimy are those of A.M. Davidson and

F.C. McGee—just two among eleven thousand, two who happened to have been celebrated hockey players. Carved into the base of the monument are words that speak to the significance of the sacrifice made by young men who were miners, or farmers, or clerks, or fishermen—or hockey players—before deciding to become Canadian soldiers:

> *To the valour of their countrymen in the Great War and in memory of their sixty thousand dead this monument is raised by the people of Canada.*

Appendix

Acknowledgements

Like my first book, *Remembered in Bronze and Stone*, the title now in your hands first saw the light of day as an illustrated presentation at an annual spring seminar of the Western Front Association—Pacific Coast Branch. The *Rinks to Regiments* presentation was enthusiastically received by my audience, particularly by John Azar, the current WFA-PCB chair. At the November 2016 launch John allowed as how the first book was all well and good but the one MacLeod should have written first is *Rinks*—let's demand he get going on it. The enduring push from John has been a factor—the leading factor—in the result that my book about hockey and war has become reality. But for John, *From Rinks to Regiments* would still be just an idea swimming around in my head.

I like to think I know more than a little about the history of hockey, but compared to my friend Roger McGuire, I am just a piker. Roger and I get together two or three times a year to talk about hockey history —and hardly anything else. Whether our meetings consume two hours or three or even more, there is never a lull in the conversation. I always come away from a session with Roger knowing more than when I went in. Roger gave the *Rinks* manuscript an attentive, assiduous reading. He made a host of useful observations and did me the great favour of pointing out missteps that would have eluded those readers who have nothing like the depth and breadth of Roger's hockey knowledge. I am highly grateful for his unmatched input.

I thank others who read and commented on the manuscript or who otherwise helped materially in transforming this book from fantasy to fact: Jim Busby, Alan Carver, Garth Christie, J.P. Fournier, Naomi Jewers, Lynn MacLean, Louise MacLean, Mary Sanseverino, John Sargent, Darcy Squires, Kevin Squires.

I wrote *Rinks* over a concentrated period in January and February of 2018. Janice Brown shares a roof with me and is therefore better aware than anyone of the intensity I invest in the writing of a book. Jan delivered a key role in the enterprise: before each day's session she listened attentively to the previous day's output. Reading my last day's work aloud delivered two benefits: voicing the writing enabled me to see ways I could strengthen it, and Jan's suggestions were helpful and almost always led to improvements. Jan did something else of consequence: left to my own devices I might go eight or ten hours without bothering to stop for food and water. Jan doesn't allow that. I am grateful for all her considerable contributions to this book.

At a time when attention spans sometimes seem limited to 140 characters, when books get far less attention than tweets, my view that publishers are unusually brave people—perhaps even reckless ones—is more entrenched than ever. I thank Rodger Touchie of Heritage House for going to the well a second time: publishing a book of mine that is not likely to be as profitable for him as Steven King's next title will doubtless be for his publisher.

I am grateful to Rodger's supportive cast at Heritage. I never doubt that senior editor Lara Kordic is in my corner; with this project Lara played a particularly helpful role, providing a sounding board on a troublesome issue and delivering assurances—at just the right time—that *Rinks* will be a winner. I am grateful to others doing their bit for the authors in the Heritage stable: copy editor Lesley Cameron; editorial coordinator Lenore Hietkamp; proofreader Stephen Harries; book designer Jacqui Thomas; marketing coordinator Leslie Kenny. Thank you all for the part you play in producing and supporting this work.

Over a period of a dozen years I have amassed an archive of hockey memorabilia on the photo-sharing web site, *Flickr*. The historical images attract thousands of views. Some of the people drawn to these collections are relatives of Hall-of-Fame players featured in *Rinks*; some add value by sharing family stories I would never otherwise know. I am particularly grateful to the families of Frank Fredrickson and Gordon "Duke" Keats for their generosity in sharing the images, photo negatives, letters, diaries, etc., that have significantly informed not just the Fredrickson and Keats sections of the book but others too. These contributions do much to enhance the impact and colour of the stories recounted here.

Sources

From Rinks to Regiments reflects my long interest in the game of hockey and its history. For six decades I have been a gatherer of hockey lore, memorabilia, images, and stories.

Among the books lining my hockey shelves, the oldest and longest-serving is *Official N.H.L. Record Book 1917–64* (Ken-Will Publishing, 1964). It is a year-by-year numbers-only account of the NHL's first forty-seven seasons: league standings, playoff results, and individual player statistics. I frequently consulted this diminutive fifty-four-year-old *Record Book* while writing this book.

Other books have been helpful in framing the times and milieu of men who were both hockey luminaries and soldiers in the war of 1914–18.

The Trail of the Stanley Cup by Charles L. Coleman (National Hockey League, 1976) is a prodigious and comprehensive three-volume history covering the first seventy-four years of the Cup, from 1893 through 1964. For hockey historians wanting to delve into every facet of the Cup's history, there is no better starting point than Coleman's masterwork. But because these volumes are cherished by hockey historians, and were never printed in large numbers, they are difficult to acquire. Individual volumes are sometimes offered for sale in Internet marketplaces at three-figure prices or more. For the reader simply wishing to examine Coleman's work, the easiest way to access it is by inter-library loan.

In *Deceptions and Doublecross: How the NHL Conquered Hockey* (Dundurn, 2002), Morey Holtzman and Joseph Nieforth offer a no-holds-barred analysis of the machinations leading to the founding of the National Hockey League and its appropriation of the Stanley Cup.

Stephen J. Harper's *A Great Game: The Forgotten Leafs and the Rise of Professional Hockey* (Simon & Schuster, 2013), focuses on the early history of hockey in Canada. It is particularly useful in illuminating the tensions that developed between entrepreneurs keen to transform hockey into a business for profit and the old guard ardent about maintaining the game's purity as a strictly amateur endeavour.

Howard Schubert's *Architecture on Ice: A History of the Hockey Arena* (McGill-Queen's University Press, 2016), is a detailed and lavishly illustrated treatment of the history of hockey arenas going back to the game's beginnings. It addresses most of the early arenas referenced in this book.

Heroes & History: Voices from NHL's Past! (McGraw-Hill Ryerson, 1994), features Stan and Shirley Fischler's interviews with "The Greats Who Are Gone," including two featured here: Cooper Smeaton and Frank Fredrickson.

The Lives of Conn Smythe: From the Battlefield to Maple Leaf Gardens, A Hockey Icon's Story, by Kelly McParland (Fenn/McLelland & Stewart, 2011), addresses the life of the man who built the Toronto Maple Leaf, including Conn Smythe's war experiences as a soldier, airman, and prisoner-of-war in Germany.

Richard Brignall's *Forgotten Heroes* (J. Gordon Shillingford Publishing, 2011), tackles the breadth and depth of hockey history in Winnipeg from 1890 to 1959. It too is generously illustrated and includes references to the players addressed in the present book who learned to skate and score in Winnipeg in the years before the Great War.

In *The Battle of Alberta: A Century of Hockey's Greatest Rivalry* (Heritage House, 2005), Steven Sandor illuminates Edmonton-Calgary hockey rivalries dating back to the 1920s, when the Edmonton Eskimos and Calgary Tigers of the Western Canada Hockey League vied for the hearts and minds of Alberta hockey fans.

Michael McKinley's *Hockey: A People's History* (McLelland & Stewart, 2006), offers more than four pounds of text and image illuminating the game from its ancient origins to the passing of Maurice "Rocket" Richard in 2000.

Harry Trihey's fury at the breakup of the 199th Battalion is discussed by Matthew Barlow in "The Montreal Shamrocks Hockey Club," published online in the *Montreal Mosaic WebMagazine* (montrealmosaic.com/article/montreal-shamrocks-hockey-club).

Cooper Smeaton's on-ice battle with Howard McNamara is a subject in Brian McFarlane's "Early Leagues and the Birth of the NHL," available on the Washington Capitals website (archive.li/2rdRH).

Duke Keats's exchange with gentlemen in the employ of the gangster Al Capone is discussed in Gordon W. Russell's *Aggression in the Sports World: A Social Psychological Perspective* (Oxford University Press, 2008).

Details in my account of Frank Fredrickson, including his 1933 association with Albert Einstein, were provided by Fredrickson's son, Bud Fredrickson, and daughter-in-law, Alixe Fredrickson.

In *Empire of Ice*, Craig H. Bowlsby (Knights of Winter, 2012) sets out a season-by-season account of the Pacific Coast Hockey Association. The PCHA founders, Lester and Frank Patrick, aimed at challenging the NHL for major league hockey supremacy. While they were at it, the two brothers introduced an array of innovations that endure to the present day. *Empire of Ice* includes useful appendices setting out league and individual player statistics.

James Duplacey and Eric Zweig's *Official Guide to the Players of the Hockey Hall of Fame* (Firefly Books, 2010) is a useful small-format compendium of player statistics and highlights of the Hall-of-Famers' careers.

Several online sources are available for those interested in researching hockey statistics—both team and individual—for the periods before and after the First World War. I recommend *Hockey Reference* (hockey-reference.com) and the *Internet Hockey Database* (hockeydb.com).

Desmond Morton's *When Your Number's Up: The Canadian Solider in the First World War* (Random House, 1993) remains the source I value most in my attempts to comprehend the experience of the ordinary soldier in the Canada Corps of 1914–18. In the present context, *When Your Number's Up* was particularly useful in enabling me to fathom the prevalence of sexually transmitted infections in the Canada Corps and the problems it posed for senior commanders.

There are several useful online resources through which to access soldiers' war records and regimental war diaries. The most important of these is Library and Archive Canada's database containing the service records of men and women who served in the Canada Corps during the war. LAC has been digitizing these records, a task now almost complete. Most of the accounts of the subjects of this book as soldiers were derived from a close reading of the service records accessed from LAC's database, *Personnel Records of the First World War* (bac-lac.gc.ca/eng/discover/military-heritage/first-world-war/personnel-records/Pages/search.aspx). The LAC also has a database, *War Diaries of the First World War*, providing access to regimental war diaries (collectionscanada.gc.ca/archivianet/02015202_e.html).

A useful guide to the ace fighter pilots of the Great War is the website *The Aerodrome: Aces and Aircraft of World War I*, published by The Aerodrome (theaerodrome.com/index.php).

For several years I have maintained an album of images and text on the photo-sharing website *Flickr*: "Hockey and the Great War." This online album attracts a good deal of traffic, some of it from relatives of Hall-of-Fame players with anecdotes to share. Some players' relatives have been particularly generous in sharing war diaries, photographs, and family stories. I pay particular tribute to these individuals in the Acknowledgements section of this book.

As for the images sprinkled throughout the book, each of them is intended to put a face to a name in the text. Some images are from my personal collection and several were given to me by the individuals thanked in the Acknowledgements.

Hockey cards—bits of stiff paper bearing the image of players—have been used to market cigarettes, candies, and bubble gum for more than a century. Many of the images used in this book are of mass-marketed hockey cards, a good number of them from my own personal collection. A small number of my own photographs of places and artefacts are also incorporated.

The remaining illustrations accompanying the text are player images—many of them available from multiple online sources—that are in the public domain.

Index

Madison Square Garden, 131
Malone, Joe, 6, 8, 34, 173
managers, 99–100, 101, 103, 105, 140
Manitoba Junior Hockey League, 87
Manitoba Senior Hockey League (MSHL), 113
Maple Leaf Gardens, 105
Maritime Professional Hockey League (MPHL), 33
Mauretania (ship), 48
McGee, Charles Edward, 12, 24, 26
McGee, Frank, 8, 11, 12, 21–28, 29, 31, 60, 171, 175
McGee, Jim, 23
McGee, Thomas D'Arcy, 23
McGee, Walter Robert, 24
McLaughlin, Frederick, 149, 150
McLaughlin, Major Frederic, 110
McNamara, George, 32–36, 58, 59, 108, 111
McNamara, Harold, 33, 36
McNamara, Howard, 32, 33, 34, 36, 47
McNaughton Cup, 93
medals, 48, 79, 89, 102, 138
Meeker, Howie, 172–73
Memorial Cup, 170–71
Metagama (ship), 138, 161
Minesing, 51
Minneapolis Millers, 162, 163
Minneapolis Rockets, 162
Montreal Canadiens, 2, 34, 47, 52, 54, 57, 67–69, 85–86, 117, 125, 126, 131, 167
Montreal Hockey Club, 19
Montreal Maroons, 80, 117, 126, 127, 136, 140, 145, 158, 168
Montreal Shamrocks, 16, 17, 18–19, 32, 32, 33, 35
Montreal St.-François-Xavier, 121, 122
Montreal Wanderers, 28–29, 30, 78
Moore, Dickie, 2
Moose Jaw Moose, 44
Moran, Paddy, 3
Morenz, Howie, 140, 163
Most Valuable Players, 68, 69, 105, 157
Mount Sorrel, battle of, 66

National Hockey Association (NHA), 9–10, 29, 34, 52, 56, 57, 60, 78, 108, 125, 131, 134
National Hockey League (NHL), 7, 10, 16, 54, 100, 125, 135, 145, 167
New Edinburghs, 134
Newfoundland Regiment, 156
New York Americans, 81, 91, 131–32, 145, 154, 163
New York Rangers, 85, 91, 99, 103, 140–41, 162–63, 172
New York St. Nicholas, 73
New York Wanderers, 47
NHL records, 8
Nighbor, Frank, 57, 173
Noble, Reg, 6, 124–27, 150, 168
North Bay Trappers, 107
Northern Michigan Senior Hockey League, 96–97

Northern Ontario Hockey Association (NOHA), 107, 121, 139

Olympic (ship), 79, 89, 130, 148
Olympic Games, 8, 64, 93, 94–95, 116, 155, 157–58
Ontario Hockey Association (OHA), 35, 39, 57, 62, 97, 101, 124, 129, 130, 154, 155–58
Ontario Hockey League, 170
Ontario Professional Hockey League (OPHL), 33
Ottawa Auditorium, 135
Ottawa Brigands, 166
Ottawa Cliffsides, 166
Ottawa Gunners, 166
Ottawa Rideau Rebels, 17
Ottawa Rough Riders, 133
Ottawa Senators, 21, 27, 28–29, 30, 68, 78–81, 90, 98, 134–36, 153, 167–68
Ottawa Silver Seven, 21–23, 28, 29

Pacific Coast Hockey Association (PCHA), 9–10, 52, 58, 78, 80, 84, 97–98
Parkdale Canoe Club, 158
Passchendaele, battle of, 12, 52, 89, 102–3, 129–30
Patrick, Frank, 9, 10, 52, 84, 98
Patrick, Lester, 3, 9, 10, 29, 52, 58, 84, 95, 103, 111, 117, 172
penalty shot introduced, 10
Penetanguishene, 32
Philadelphia Quakers, 49–50
Pittsburgh Pirates, 118
Port Arthur Bearcats, 121, 122
Port Arthur Ports, 122
Port Arthur Shuniahs, 119
Port Arthur War Vets, 120
Port Colborne Sailors, 154
Portland Rosebuds, 82, 84, 149
Princess Patricia's Canadian Light Infantry, 144
Princeton Tigers, 73
Princeton University, 118

Quebec Bulldogs, 8, 34, 131
Queen's University, 19, 37–39, 42, 171

Rankin, Frank, 50, 157
Rankin, Frank Gilchrist, 61–64
referees, 19, 31, 45, 46–50, 127, 136
Regina Capitals, 67, 84, 148
Regina Victorias, 83, 88–89, 148–49, 157
Renfrew Creamery Kings, 9, 9
Richard, Maurice "The Rocket," 61, 64, 85
Richardson, George, 37–42, 57, 59, 171
Richardson, James, 42
Rickard, Tex, 103
rovers, 8–9, 17, 62
Royal Canadians, 134
Royal Flying Corps, 53, 102, 114, 156
Russell, MB, 142–43
Russian expeditionary force, 138–39, 165
Ruttan, Jack, 7, 43–45

Sarnia Sailors, 97
Saskatchewan Senior Hockey League, 83, 148
Saskatoon Crescents, 140
Saskatoon Sheiks, 139–40
Sault Ste. Marie Greyhounds, 36, 139
Schmidt, Milt, 172
Seattle Metropolitans, 52, 80, 135
Second World War, 105, 118, 146, 171–72
Selkirk Fishermen, 88, 90
Selkirk Steelers, 87
Shirriff hockey coins, 2
Siberia (expeditionary force), 138–39, 165
Simpson, "Bullet" Joe, 87–91, 110, 131
Sittler, Darryl, 8
Smeaton, Cooper, 46–50, 118
Smiths Falls Seniors, 27–28
Smythe, Conn, 85, 101–5, 140, 172
Smythe, Stafford, 105
Somme, battle of the, 25, 89, 102, 156
Southern Alberta Senior Hockey (SASH) League,
   57
Southern California Hockey League, 163
Spanish influenza, 13, 18, 148
Stanley, Arthur and Edward, 16, 17
Stanley Cup, background, 7, 8, 10; playoffs,
   16, 19, 22, 28–29, 52, 54, 78, 80, 84, 85–86,
   97, 98, 99, 100, 103, 105, 107, 117, 126, 131,
   135, 141, 153, 163, 167, 168; professional-only
   trophy, 36, 121; trustee, 50, 145
STDs, 13, 79, 89, 161
Stephen (ship), 138
St. Julien, battle of, 39–40
St. Louis Eagles, 136
St. Michael's College, 124
St. Paul Athletic Club, 93, 94
St. Paul Saints, 95
Stratford, 62, 64, 150
Sudbury All-Stars, 129
Sudbury Wolves, 130–31
Sweden (team), 64, 93, 116, 158
Switzerland (team), 93, 158

Taylor, Cyclone, 3
Thunder Bay Senior Hockey League, 107, 119,
   120, 122
Toronto Arenas, 6, 97, 125–26
Toronto Argonauts, 151
Toronto Aura Lee, 151, 156
Toronto Blueshirts, 27, 35, 52, 56–59, 63, 107–9,
   124–25
Toronto Dentals, 156
Toronto Eaton's, 62
Toronto Granites, 63–64, 157
Toronto Hockey Club, 34
Toronto Maple Leafs, 8, 85, 94, 99, 102, 103–4,
   105, 150, 154, 168, 173
Toronto Marlboros, 158
Toronto Nationals, 158
Toronto National Sea Fleas, 158–59
Toronto Riversides, 124

Toronto Shamrocks, 27
Toronto St. Andrew's, 155–56
Toronto St. Michael's, 62
Toronto St. Patricks, 80, 98, 103, 126, 152–53,
   154
Toronto Tecumsehs, 34
Toronto Varsity Grads, 121
Trihey, Harry, 7, 16–20, 22, 60

unions, 99–100, 105, 131
University of British Columbia, 118
University of Manitoba, 43–45, 113, 144
University of Ottawa, 73
University of Saskatchewan, 63, 64, 157
University of Toronto, 116, 121
University of Toronto Schools, 170
USA (team), 94–95, 116, 158, 159
US Amateur Hockey Association, 162

Vancouver Millionaires, 78, 80, 84, 97, 98, 126,
   153
Victoria Aristocrats, 58, 59
Victoria Cougars, 53, 80, 99, 117, 126, 131
Vimy Ridge, 4, 12, 25, 26, 52, 144, 174–75

Waterloo Colts, *32*, 33
Watson, Harry Ellis, 8, 155–59
Western Canada Hockey League (WCHL), 10,
   67, 80, 84, 90, 99, 103, 109, 139, 145, 149
Western Hockey League, 103, 117, 127
Whitby Athletics, 155
Wilson, Gordon Allan "Phat," 7, 119–22
Windsor Spitfires, 170
Winnipeg, 43–44
Winnipeg Falcons, 113, 115–16
Winnipeg Hockey Club, 44
Winnipeg Merchant's Bank, 65, 66
Winnipeg Military Hockey League, 45
Winnipeg Monarchs, 82, 88, 147, 162
Winnipeg Northern Crowns, 65
Winnipeg Selkirks, 130
Winnipeg Somme, 45, 83
Winnipeg Strathconas, 82, 88, 147
Winnipeg Victorias, 19, 65, 88
Winnipeg Vimy, 45, 83
Winnipeg Ypres, 45, 83

YMCA, 96
Ypres, Third Battle of, 129–30

About the Author

Alan Livingstone MacLeod has a lifelong passion for history and writing. Since retiring from the field of labour relations, he has transformed his passion into two books and a number of public lectures commemorating Canadian efforts in the First World War. His first book, *Remembered in Bronze and Stone: Canada's Great War Memorial Statuary*, was published in 2016.